8 DAYS

JESSICA
LOCKWOOD

8 DAYS

If you follow the pattern of the sun each night from the same perspective for one year, you will notice that its position forms an elongated infinity symbol. In astrology this phenomenon is called an analemma, two rings that form the number eight. Eight, the astral number symbolizing infinity, is all the days of matrimony that the stars blessed Chason and I with. Had I known we'd only have eight days, I still wouldn't have changed a thing. Every moment was perfect. Until it wasn't.

We married on June 9, 2021. He drowned in the Crystal River on June 17, 2021. We were only married for 8 days. 8, the symbol for infinity, is how I like to think of our love. Infinite and everlasting.

The first ring that Chason gave me was simple: a sunstone, neatly placed in a simple band. He proposed on a beach in Baja, Mexico, and said he wanted me to design my real engagement ring when we got back to Colorado from our mini vacation.

My mother and father had been separated for almost two years, and my mother asked if I'd like to take her wedding ring and make it my own. It was originally my great grandmother's ring, from my father's side. I appreciated the gesture and accepted the gift.

I took that family ring and deconstructed it. The design was simple. I took one diamond from the ring and set it horizontally, aligning it perfectly onto a rose gold band. I used the other diamonds to make a set of earrings for my mother, with the intention of gifting them to her on the eve of our big day. The plan was to elope, then say our vows in front of all our friends and family the following fall.

When Chason and I exchanged rings, at the John Denver Park in Aspen on the day of our elopement, he gave me a wedding band encircled with tiny raw diamonds. I had chosen each stone with care, to reflect all the different shades of olive green I saw when I looked into Chason's eyes.

I wanted to save the heirloom diamond band for the big day when we said our vows in front of all our friends and family, a year later. Unfortunately that day never came, and instead I put that ring on my finger the morning of Chason's memorial.

I wear the three rings together as a set—on my right ring finger, not my left. I want to keep my heart open because I believe Chason would not want me to be alone for my remaining days. He died at the age of 41, and I became a widow at 39. Life is short, but life is also long. One of life's many paradoxes.

CHAP
1

WEDDING DAY: JUNE 9TH, 2021

I will not die an unlived life.
I will not live in fear of falling
or catching fire.
I choose to inhabit my days,
To allow my living to open me,
To make me less afraid,
More accessible,
To loosen my heart
Until it becomes a wing,
A torch, a promise.
I choose to risk my significance;
To live so that which came to me as a seed
Goes to the next as blossom
And that which came to me as blossom
goes on as fruit.

—Dawna Markova

YOU ARE CORDIALLY UN-INVITED

We had chosen hump day to say our "I do's." Wednesday, June 9, 2021. 6/9. The symbol of yin and yang. A consummate of Chason and me. Two opposites, eternally connected. Me a Virgo and Chason a Pisces, opposites on the zodiac calendar. Virgos are earth signs, dedicated to service and pragmatism. Pisces are water signs, empathetic and capable of blessing all those around them. Both are powerful healers.

I ironed Chason's shirt the evening before we tied the knot. He borrowed it from a friend and brought it home accordioned and messy. It fit nicely before the iron pressed out the wrinkles. The day we married, we woke and we dressed. He commented that his newly ironed shirt was now too big, and that it made him feel small. But there was no time to waste. He buttoned it up, threw on his finest pair of jeans, cinched up his belt, and found his cleanest flat-brimmed hat. He smiled at me, then winked. Skinny-strong, I thought, as I looked at him across the room in admiration.

I slipped on a little white tea dress that I had stumbled upon just a few days prior while shopping for a get-well gift for our friend, Cat. Stan, her husband, had convinced her to join him on a river trip down the Grand Canyon but it had not gone as planned. She shattered her wrist riding rodeo down Horn Rapid and had to be medically evacuated just days into their three-week trip. But now, with Cat and Stan both home early, we had witnesses for our spontaneous nuptials.

Cat-n-Stan, not to be confused with some epic, faraway land, met us outside the Aspen Court House. The morning was bright, and the air was crisp. Cat, on the ready, brought me a bouquet of ranunculus and thistle. The soft petals and thorny prickles seemed symbolic for our budding love. Beautiful, yet dangerous.

We recited, we signed, we notarized, we kissed.

Marriage license in hand, we walked the paths of John Denver Park. The trails were sweetly caressed by high river flows. Fragrant lilacs were in full bloom and the buzz of bees harmonized with the melodies of the Roaring Fork River.

We stumbled upon a hidden rocky alcove and decided it was the perfect spot to exchange our rings. We were making big mountain promises that day.

"Will you marry me, and love me forever?" Chason asked nervously, as he slid a ring of raw rocks onto my left finger.

"Even better," I replied, "I'll even let you go kayaking." Then I hesitated. "But only when it's safe."

"Only when it's safe," he sang back as he leaned in for a smooch.

"Document that!" Chason said, turning towards Stan and pointing down towards my newly wed finger.

"Don't worry Chase-Dawg, I got it on tape!" Stan replied, with a shit-eating grin.

After we exchanged rings, we traded our wedding attire for PFDs and paddles. We decided to seal the deal with a quick backyard lap down the Roaring Fork.

"Raaaaaafting!" Chason mocked as he shoved us off the shore.

"Low Expectations," I said jovially.

"Keep 'em low, babe!" he joked back.

Low Expectations was the motto of our relationship, and the name of our nine-foot Mini-Me, a miniature version of a real-size raft. We named her after a solo trip we'd done down the Lower Dolores River a few years back. At first we thought we'd call her *Divorce Boat*, but we ended up doing pretty well, so *Low Expectations* stuck and we never looked back.

After a backyard run down the Woody Creek stretch on the Roaring Fork River, we traded the Mini-Me for a full-size rig. A 15-foot oar boat that would be our vessel of burning love for our honeymoon expedition down Cataract Canyon. But before heading to Moab, for the Potash Put-in, we had to make a pit-stop in Telluride to pick up a motor.

Telluride, Colorado, is where Chason was from, and where I had lived, off and on, for over 15 years. We rolled into town at dusk and caught last light, just in time to consummate our marriage with a classic Main Street "Just Married" kiss. We were trying to be clandestine, but instead we were quite the sight. We bumped into a friend, who captured our smooch with Ajax Mountain standing proudly in the background and Ingram Falls gushing big waterfall flows. The sky was lit and there was fire on the mountain. After a brief meet-up with Chason's folks and a dinner crash from some close friends, we toasted each other and called it the perfect first night.

CHASON MY NORTH STAR

We were still planning a real wedding with all the bells and whistles. The big day was scheduled for Wednesday, September 14, 2022. It would be perfect. We had all the details ironed out: an intimate ceremony at the backcountry hut Chason's father had built deep in the San Juan Mountains at the Alta Lakes Observatory. We would have a big party afterwards in the town of Ophir, a small mountain hamlet just outside Telluride. Then we'd have all weekend to celebrate with our friends and family at the Telluride Blues and Brews Festival, in Telluride's Town Park.

On a whim, we decided to elope just three months after Chason proposed. It seemed like a great idea in the face of planning a big wedding. The guest list was getting longer by the day, and the idea of a big wedding was daunting. We were also planning a rebuild on our house—and we were trying to have a baby. Combining finances was a necessity to get the construction loan rolling, so we decided, "*Eff-it*. Let's just do it. Let's make it legal. And let's do it on the river!"

We each had a week off in June where we could steal away. We vaguely talked about a self-support-raft trip down Cataract Canyon, then thought, "Why don't we just get married the day before, then honeymoon on the river after?"

We had it all figured out. We would exchange our vows on Cataract Canyon at the Center of the Universe, where the Green River meets the Colorado River. Cataract is a 2,000 foot canyon that travels roughly 96 river miles, through Canyonlands National Park, just outside of Moab, Utah. There are 29 rapids in a 15-mile stretch, book-ended by 80 miles of serene flatwater. The beauty is palpable. Burnt clay cliffs tower high above the river, exposing the Paradox Formation, a geological wonder that ages back over three hundred million years ago. Saltcedar tamarisks, adorned with their pinkish hued blooms, line the shores, while trills of crickets incessantly buzz. Thunderous echoes of moving water lurk around every corner, leaving you feeling the true power and force of the river.

Historically, Cataract has run as big as 114,000 cubic feet per second (cfs), with an average spring runoff of about 30,000 to 50,000 cfs. The river was running super low that year at 7,000 cfs and was steadily dropping. With lazy river flows, and a motor assist, we allowed the river to take us seven days from the Potash Put-In to the Dirty Devil Take-Out. This left us with plenty of time to connect. Both with the canyon, and with each other.

CHAP

2

DAY ONE: JUNE 10TH, 2021

Patience Dear One.
Take pause.
Much like when planting a garden,
you must first break open the root ball.
This dismantlement optimizes
the potential for growth,
and allows for expansion into new soils.
Nurture this integration.
Remember chaos breeds creation.
Maintain faith that one day
the network will heal itself.
Future harvests await.
Patience, dear one.
All in divine timing.

ONCE IN A LIFETIME

After a stay in the honeymoon suite at the historic New Sheridan Hotel in downtown Telluride, where Chason's parents also spent their first night of matrimony, Chason and I ate brunch with our besties and opened small tokens for our trip. We were headed to the Center of the Universe, to recite our vows and make big mountain promises. A real elopement. Just us. No one else in sight.

We muscled the wily motor into the back of our truck, then got on the road in a flash. Arriving at the put-in midday, we rigged in high winds and pushed off at last light. The canyon turned pitch black, elucidating the Milky Way big and bright. We watched as the Arietid meteor shower illuminated the night. A proverbial rice toss, electrifying our moonless honeymoon.

It all seemed so magical, and as we floated, I couldn't help but hear David Byrne whisper into my ear,

And you may find yourself living in a shotgun shack
And you may find yourself in another part of the world
And you may find yourself behind the wheel of a large automobile
And you may find yourself in a beautiful house, with a beautiful wife
And you may ask yourself, 'Well, how did I get here?'
Letting the days go by, let the water hold me down
Letting the days go by, water flowing underground
Into the blue again after the money's gone
Once in a lifetime, water flowing underground

In the twenty years I'd been in Colorado, I'd known Chason for fifteen. Chasing whitewater, and skiing mountains all over the world, we had adventured together both as friends, and as lovers. He knew my family, and I knew his. But this was our first trip together as man and wife. And as we made our way down the river, I couldn't help but think to myself, "My God, how did *we* get here?"

LIFE'S A GARDEN, DIG IT?

I had no idea what I was in for when I left the shores of Lake Erie for the majestic Colorado Rockies. I was nineteen years old when I decided to leave blustery Buffalo for the mountains. I was raised in the Rust Belt. Not much sparkle there back in those days. I knew a lot about snow and how to fare through the long winters, but knew very little about how to fare in the mountains. Culture shock was an understatement.

Upon arriving in Boulder in 2001, I found myself living in a full house with my childhood best friend Valerie and some of her friends from the University of Colorado. One of my roommates, a guy named Buck, was born and raised in Telluride. I had never heard of the place, but was intrigued when he talked on and on about the mountains there.

Our stint in Boulder was short lived, and after only eight months on the Front Range, Val and I decided to move to southwest Colorado, to the San Juan Mountains. We had heard so much about them, we felt it was time we checked them out ourselves. I attended classes at Fort Lewis College in Durango and worked as a lift attendant at Purgatory Ski Resort.

It was a wild ride down there. I started to get my bearings and was beginning to learn how to ski in the champagne powder. The San Juans were really something. Living, working and playing in them made me start to feel like I was growing into a real mountain woman. But in 2002 and 2003, wildfires began to plague the southwest, and in the fall of 2003, Val and I decided to move back to the Front Range to take refuge from the smoke and ash.

I had made a promise to my mother before I left Buffalo that I would graduate from college. So before we left Durango, I signed up for classes at Metropolitan State University of Denver, with the intention of graduating with a business degree. Valerie was going to move in with her new boyfriend, Daniel, and it was going to be a big transition for me—the first time I would be living alone. I found myself a one-bedroom apartment in an old Victorian in the Cheesman Park neighborhood. The rent was reasonable, and I was close to campus. I dropped all my savings on first, last, and deposit, then began moving in my marginal amount of belongings.

I had some time to kill before school started and the solitude left me feeling uncomfortable. It was the first time in my life that I'd been truly alone with my thoughts. A toxic narrative, one that I had buried deep down, began to creep into the forefront of my mind. As events from my past began to present themselves, it was becoming apparent that I still had a lot of unpacking to do.

The silence that came with living alone was a new experience. My home growing up in Buffalo was loud and volatile. My mom and dad were seventeen and eighteen when they got pregnant with me. My siblings Kevin, Elizabeth, and Michael arrived shortly after, all of us three years apart.

My dad, Jim Lockwood, who stands 6 feet, 9 inches tall, was an Ironworker. Always wearing the same 42x42 Carhartt overalls, with the arms cut off his T-shirt, exposing his full sleeve tattoos, he's a real sight. He stomps around in size 14 EE Red Wing boots, which he sports half laced. The bottoms of his oversized overalls are usually bungied at the ankles so they don't get caught up in his motorcycle. My dad rode with the Outlaws. A rival to the Hell's Angels. A biker through and through. In his younger years he was a heavy drinker and rarely came home, and when he did, we'd all wished he just stayed out. His violent rants frequently led to verbal or sometimes physical blows.

My mom, Lori, was the youngest of eight children. She fell deeply in love with my father when she was in the eleventh grade. Her long strawberry blonde hair and freckled skin make her look younger than her years. She was 28 years old, and I was 9, when my youngest brother Michael was born. I could tell that the burdens of motherhood were beginning to take their toll, and decided to make it a life goal to be childless until her age, shortly after my youngest brother arrived.

Being the oldest sibling was exhausting and as an excuse to get out of the house, I found myself playing volleyball year round with my best friend Valerie. Her father was our coach and he drove us all over Western New York and Northern Pennsylvania to play in scrimmages and tournaments. In the seventh grade, the two of us signed up for Ski Club and she quickly became my life anchor.

Now, living alone for the first time in my life, the silence was becoming unbearable. I began to feel depressed. I had been using other people's presence as a distraction, using the chaos as a means to avoid dealing with my own personal issues. A flood of emotions came barreling down on me without warning, and I felt like I was headed down shit's creek without a paddle. I was all alone, without a life preserver, and I had zero coping skills to deal to the rush of emotions deluging my brain.

I didn't have the tools to recognize, nor did I have the words to describe what I was experiencing. The only adjectives I had in my emotional vocabulary at this point in my adulthood were mad, sad, glad, and rad. I was in the midst of a total breakdown, and I'd never felt so lost or alone in my entire life.

The disturbing thoughts that ran through my head were incessant. I was perseverating on a rhetoric I'd heard my father say to me, over and over again. It was toxic, harmful, shameful, volatile, and demoralizing.

You worthless piece of shit. You spoiled brat. His latest supportive words had been, *I don't even know why you're wasting your time with college. You won't be trained in anything to make a real living, and you'll only be in debt after you graduate. I say burn 'em all down. Burn all those fucking colleges down.*

The shame and guilt and disgust from my past piled on, and as the days went on I stopped eating. Anger grew, both towards myself and towards my parents. I was mad at my mom for staying with my father and allowing him to treat us, and her, like that. And I was angry at my dad for treating us as poorly as his own dad had treated him.

Why am I feeling all of this? And why now? I thought moving away would make all of this better.

I felt like a woman without a country. Each day of solitude, I spiraled further and further into a deep state of depression. I found myself losing motivation to go outside, until one day I realized I hadn't left my bed for almost a week. I began having dark thoughts about ending my miserable life, and knew I needed to get out of the house to shake them. I called Val and asked if she would meet me out in the mountains in a place called Parmalee Gulch. It was a park we used to hike when we lived in Boulder, and a place that brought me comfort in times of distress.

As we walked, I told Valerie a little about what was going on. She listened while I confided. Having someone to soundboard provided me with some relief. I had been doing life with Valerie since I was 12 years old. She knew all of my secrets. All of them, except one, and I wasn't sure how to approach it, or even where to begin.

I had been experiencing suicidal ideation since my early adolescent years. Though I never acted on the thoughts, they'd plagued me since my earliest days of high school. Valerie knew how hostile my household had been growing up, and she had witnessed some of the behaviors I was subject to. But I couldn't explain the depths of hopelessness and despair I was experiencing, because I had neither the words nor the capacity. No one had ever taught me any words to describe my feelings, and my inability to express my thoughts and emotions only made me feel more isolated.

Strolling along the singletrack, I began to come out of the sensory deprivation I'd been experiencing in my quiet, unfurnished apartment. As I began to hear the birds and chipmunks, I began to breathe a little easier. The trees around me and the duff at my feet brought me solace. The smell of pine needles and the breeze on my cheeks began to soften the tightness in my throat and chest. Nature was doing her magic and the medicine was starting to take its effect.

The more we walked, the more I felt inspired. The mountains offered me a new way of healing that I couldn't explain to my friends and family back home. *I had tried, but they didn't understand.* By the time we got back to our cars, I had devised a plan. It had come from a place of scarcity, but my new idea brought a feeling of abundance. I was going to start a window garden in my new apartment. If I learned how to grow my own food, I would never go hungry. It was a presumptuous idea, since I had never grown anything before in my life, but it offered me some hope and some relief.

"I'm gonna stop at a garden store on my way home and pick up some pots and some dirt," I told Valerie. "I'll put it on my new credit card," I said, reassuring myself that I could pay it off later, when I got my first paycheck. "I'll buy some seeds and plant some food in the window box, at my new place."

Valerie just looked at me puzzled. "Yeah, okay. I bet you have a great window for a project like that."

"It gets great morning light, and I think food will grow there," I said, shocking both myself and Val with this unusual plan.

She looked at me, slightly confused, but I felt reassured that this do-it-yourself project would get me out of my slump. I needed something to nurture and I had an inkling that the plants would make great roommates. Quiet and clean.

I stopped at the garden store and picked up my supplies. When I got home I dumped the dirt into pots, dusting perlite and moss all over the floor. I had no idea how large any of the plants were going to get, so I followed the instructions on the back of the seed packets.

I plunked green bean seed pods into a neat little row, then patted down the dirt. Then, I sprinkled lettuce seeds onto a large rectangular tray, and gently brushed them into the soil with my fingers. I soaked nasturtium seeds overnight, then placed them deep into the corners of a circular pot. Then I dropped one single squash seed in the center. I arranged the pots and the lettuce tray in the window box, then watered and waited for them to grow.

I don't know what inspired the project. An inner knowing, I suppose, and the task left me feeling invigorated and hopeful. I didn't grow up gardening. I grew up in the kitchen making food, feeding kids and doing dishes. The urge to plant vegetables came from outta nowhere, a bolt of inspiration that hit me on the dirt path. Planting seeds gave me purpose and the dirt grounded me.

As the punishing monologue retreated, I had a new grip on how to handle my victim narrative. My shame seemed to fall away with the possibility of new growth. Classes were about to begin, and I was on my way to earning a degree, with or without my father's blessing. It felt like a fresh start.

SAFETY THIRD

I made a new friend while living in Denver. His name was Logan, and he worked as a raft guide during the summer months down in Cañon City on the Royal Gorge of the Arkansas River. He was good friends with Valerie's boyfriend Daniel and he often invited us on fun adventures down the Arkansas. One day he asked if I'd like to go R2'ing with him.

It's a funny thing, rafting. When you get introduced to the sport, it's like learning a whole new language. I had no idea what R2'ing meant, but I trusted Logan. He was a seasoned raft guide and a big-water kayaker, so I loaded up my truck with some camping gear and jumped on board.

When I got to the boathouse I was greeted by a bunch of dirtbag river rats. *My kind of people*, I thought. Everyone was hanging out and tallying up beer fines from the day's thrills and spills.

Some guys were throwing rafts onto a trailer and asked if I would grab some paddles, then help schlep the rest of the gear into a beat-up van. I tackled the task, then found a life jacket that fit. We piled into the van, then headed to the put-in. When we got to the river, I noticed that the rafts we were unloading were much smaller than the rafts I remembered taking down before, when I had gone rafting with Logan.

That's when I realized I needed a little more beta on what we were about to do.

"So, what's the story with these tiny boats?" I asked as casually as I could.

Logan explained that the rafts were nine feet long, much smaller than the 14- or 16-foot rafts they usually took down the river.

That's when I noticed that there were a lot of rafts, and not a lot of people to paddle them.

"Sooo, how many people go in each boat?" I asked with a confused and slightly terrified look on my face.

That's when he explained that we would be R2'ing.

Again, I needed clarification.

"Yeah, I told you, we're R2'ing. It's just you and me!"

"Soooo, R2 Means two paddlers. Ok, wow. Now I get it!" I was completely gripped.

Perplexed at how foolish I must have been to have agreed to this adventure, I buckled up my life jacket and found a paddle. I was super green, and super freaked out.

The previous times we'd gone down the river, Logan had rowed us down in an oar rig. I just sat there, looking like a Bow Betty, on the front of his raft.

But now here I was at the put-in, standing in my "custy" PFD—another new word I had just learned, which meant customer personal flotation device—silently freaking out.

There was no turning back. The shuttle van was long gone.

So the plan was for the two of us to forge down the meaty Class IV section of whitewater one paddle stroke at a time. Logan steering the wheel and me powering the engine, so to speak.

The only thing 'extreme' about my abilities for this adventure were my extremely novice paddle strokes. I had no time to respond, I was in full panic mode.

Logan cracked open a beer and dove straight into a swift-water safety talk.

After we each took a hit off a spliff, "Safety Third" was all I really caught of the talk, and down the river we went.

Logan showed me the proper way to hold my paddle, went over a couple paddle commands, then showed me how to perform each stroke. I felt like I was drinking from a fire hose, water pouring out of my ears. Every word he said, and every paddle stroke he showed me was completely foreign.

I was totally out of my element.

I took a few gulps from my frosty cold snack, hoping for a little liquid courage, then hopped into the boat, and found my footing. The small craft we were in was called a Mini-me. It was dark green, and I couldn't help but think to myself, "How the hell did I get myself into this pickle?!"

There's a certain team-building dynamic to R2'ing that teaches the paddler the true power of each stroke. The goal is to tee up to each wave and punch through the coursing current. If you are not in unison, you will turn the boat and get crushed by the wave. Having spatial awareness in the raft is also very important. You sit super close to your partner, so you don't want to punch them in the face while you're getting tossed around in the middle of a rapid.

Finding a good paddle partner is like finding a suitable spouse. It takes a huge amount of trust, communication, and patience. As with tandem canoeing, another common name for R-2'ing is "divorce boating."

Logan and I successfully made it through the crux rapid, Sunshine Falls, and I was loving the ride. We were crushing it. Mostly because he was super good at barking out orders. And because I was so gripped, I obeyed like a good dog.

I was learning how to paddle whitewater, and the excitement from the rapids made me feel alive. After a complex rapid, I'd look back at the mess of rocks and holes upstream and feel empowered by my capacity to make it through.

I became curious. *What would life look like if I became a raft guide? Could I even do it?* Life on the river was appealing. There was a certain draw that came from the currents down below. There was a sense of family-like camaraderie that came with figuring out river logistics. It seemed like a simple and affordable way to live.

I started hanging out at the boathouse more and more. Kind of like a Penny Lane, but instead of hanging out with rock stars, I was hanging out with dirtbag raft guides.

When the clients drove away, it was our time to play. Five o'clock was the guides' put-in time, a golden hour when the sun begins to set and the moon light shines the way.

I loved being on the water at night. The stars offered a new perspective, and the moon showed me the ways of the current. The incandescent reflection illuminated the eddies and taught me the lines through complex rapids. I learned how to surrender to the flow instead of trying to fight the current. I was introduced to the fine art of finessing the skull and started to get the drift. The river inspired me to appreciate the journey, and to let go of the destination.

INDECISION ROCK

The Arkansas is a dam-fed river supplied by the run-off from the Holy Cross and Elk Mountain Ranges. It was the start of fall 2004, and the river was beginning to shut down. I was feeling bummed that the season on the Ark was winding down. Logan and I were a few beers in, and I somehow got talked into paddling a Class V section on the headwaters of the Colorado.

I'd never been on the infamous river. I had never run Class V before. But I didn't want to miss out on my chance to run the mighty Colorado. An event was being held up in Gore Canyon, the epitome of Class V whitewater. I was lacking experience, and my naiveté got the best of me. I accepted the invite, and headed over to Rancho del Rio, a campground on the Upper Colorado River where a large group of kayakers and rafters were gearing up for the annual race. I was assured that there would be plenty of safety boaters in the water, making this the perfect time to run this challenging section.

I went with Logan and our friend Orion, which meant we were an R3—but because of fluctuating river levels, my friends wanted to recruit another paddler to make us a stronger R4 paddle crew. There was a pretty big party happening in the parking lot at the Rancho del Rio, the night before the race, and my comrades were sure we would find someone to fill the spot.

"Come hell or high water, we'll find our fourth paddler," Logan reassured me.

But by the time morning rolled around, a bohemian wild man swinging a samurai sword and walking around with no shoes was our only candidate. To make matters worse, I'd been eaten alive by red ants the night before at the campground. I woke up with a swollen right eye and a fat lower lip. We found our way to the Campground General Store and I swallowed some Benadryl to relieve the histamine fit that was ensuing on my face. The medication made me drowsy, and a fresh hatch of butterflies began fluttering around in my hungover belly. My nerves were on edge, but were tempered by the groggy side effects from the med. Not a good combo.

I could have backed out, but I never found the words. I didn't say a peep, as Logan prepared me for the new set of paddle commands I needed to know before going down this next level of whitewater. Never having seen Class V, I had no idea what kind of adventure I was getting myself into, but judging by the energy at the campground before we ran shuttle, I could tell it was going to be BIG!

We rolled out our 14-foot raft and started to pump it up. We threw it onto a fully loaded trailer, then headed upriver towards the put-in. Logan helped me into my PFD. I cinched down my helmet and gripped the T-handle of my paddle. I was holding on so hard, you could see the whites of my knuckles. I wanted to make sure I wasn't going to lose it, as it was the only thing that was gonna keep me in the boat, according to Logan's latest safety talk.

There was no mention of "safety third" in this new version, only "Don't lose your paddle!"

There was a long, three-mile section of flatwater before the river made its way into the dark gorge. Logan was calling out paddle commands, getting the four of us in sync before we dropped into the canyon. Anxiety had caught my tongue, and my throat became stiff and dry. I still couldn't find the words to ask what I had gotten myself into, and it didn't matter anyway, because soon enough, a horizon line began to form, off into the distance. Spray from the rapid's splashes danced along the river's edge. A roar began to rumble, and I could see the canyon walls begin to rise high into the indigo blue Coloradoan sky. The water began to move faster, as the green tongue began to sweep our boat quickly into the current.

We were approaching Applesauce Falls, the first of nine rapids on the expert-level stretch of whitewater. We tee'd up our nimble little boat into the entrance of the canyon, as waves beat down on us every which way. We muscled our way through the first big drop with vigor, and before I knew it, we had made our way through its gates.

After we completed the entrance exam rapid, we were greeted by a team of paddlers, all dressed in matching outfits, perched high on a large rock in the dead center of the next big rapid.

A crowd of racers and safety kayakers were lined up on the shores of the river yelling, "STOP!" while doing the universal hand gesture for "DANGER AHEAD!" Luckily we had enough time and strength to eddy out, river right, before the next big rapid began.

A professional paddle team had wrapped their shiny new raft on a large obstacle famously known as Indecision Rock. Their indecision put them in between a rock and a hard place, no doubt about that.

The safety crew, who were all sporting bright orange safety vests, were devising a plan to dislodge the wrapped vessel, using a 3 point Z-drag system. I had never seen this type of rescue before, and the logistics took me by surprise.

In short, the Z-drag is a 3:1 mechanical advantage system that uses a rope, carabiners, pulleys, webbing, and prusik cording to move a heavy boat off an obstacle. Logan explained it to me like this: "Imagine you have a 100-pound bucket of cement. When you grab the handle, you'll struggle to lift it, because your arm is lifting all 100 pounds. But if a friend grabs onto the handle with you, you will each only be lifting 50 pounds. Add another and you'll each be lifting a third. Three arms makes for light work, hence the 3:1 system."

I was intrigued by the ingenuity of the system. I knew nothing about rafting, and even less about the safety involved in the sport. The more I learned, the less I knew. And the more I wanted to know.

We sat and watched as the rescuers struggled to dislodge the raft from Indecision, until finally the rope snapped and the whole system went awry. The safety crew decided to start sending rafts down the river to collect the stranded paddle crew one by one off the rock. It was the most reasonable thing to do at this point, which meant the professional team would have to leave their shiny new raft behind.

I was stunned that this pro paddle team had gotten themselves into such a predicament. And even more shocked, that I, a complete novice, was about to forge into the abyss of this class V section of rapids and waterfalls without even owning my own PFD.

Why am I here, in a place where matchy-match professionals can't even manage to maneuver their craft without casualties? Seriously, what had I gotten myself into?

We loaded back up into our old borrowed commercial raft as Logan barked out commands.

"All forward! STOP! Draw right! STOP! Right back! STOP! All forward!"

All I could do was listen and follow directions. Logan was like a drill sergeant in the stern of the raft, ruddering us to and fro as we powered our way through the mighty rapids.

Nothing else matters while you are in the thick of it. All you can do is stick your paddle into the water and make purchase with every wave. Everything else in life just falls to the wayside. In all the chaos, the world becomes still. There is no turning back once you've committed to the ripple.

Maybe that's the lure? Once you're in, you're in. Totally committed.

Before I knew it, we were passing Indecision, and a matchy-match paddler jumped off of the rock and landed smack dab in the middle of our little raft as we skirted by their raft-wrapped entanglement.

We eddied out after the last big drop, then ditched the matchy-match with his other teammates.

There are a set of railroad tracks that run alongside the river's edge. The DQ'd profesh team were going to have to huff it on foot, while the rest of us continued our way down the meaty mess that makes up Gore Canyon.

The next big obstacle was Tunnel Falls, a 14-foot waterfall. Logan lined us up for the drop as we all took one last paddle stroke before the water cascades over the falls. As I leaned back to brace for the impact, I saw Logan launch through the air, then punch the back of Orion's helmet with his left fist.

Like a barrel over Niagara, the raft slammed into the aerated bubbles down below. Thankfully the river let us go. Logan collected himself in the front of the boat, then scurried back to the stern just in time to make the next big move.

We all began to shout when we realized that we had made it over the falls safely. I looked back at Logan, his hand busted open, dripping blood all over the boat, and a smear of red, like war paint, adorning his face.

An homage, I thought, to the river gods for safe passage. He threw up the universal hand gesture for devil's horns, then gave us the signature Gene Simmons tongue while yelling,

"Fuck yeah, Gore Canyon! Fuck, yeah! AAARRRGGGHHH!"

We all raised our paddles and did a team high five. I was slightly horrified by the whole scene, and extremely happy to have made it over the falls without injury, though I was astonished and bewildered by its force. We made it to the take-out in one piece and on our way back to the flatwater, I thought to myself, "I am in no rush to boat Class V again."

I LIVE IN A SHASTA, DOWN BY THE RIVER

I didn't have any serious career plans after I walked across the stage at Metro State in May 2005, and decided to give river guiding a try after I graduated with my *"useless"* business degree, as my dad had put it.

Logan had told me about a training program on the Ark, further upstream in a town called Buena Vista. It was being held on a much easier stretch of river known as Brown's Canyon. It would be a great place for me to get my bearings and teach me how to safely navigate the river.

My Gore Canyon experience must have earned me some river cred. I interviewed over the phone and was offered a spot on the rookie training roster. I was psyched for the opportunity. It was going to be a new north star for me. I was leaving the Front Range and moving back to the mountains, to the heart of Colorado.

It would be too *intense* to sleep *in tents* all summer, so before the river season started, I headed back to Buffalo to pick up an old family heirloom, the 1957 Shasta. It was a tow-behind camper I had grown up camping in with my family. My father agreed to give it to me for my latest adventure as a raft guide. He welded a hitch onto my truck so I could tow it out from New York to Colorado. A mechanic once told me that if I ever lost the camper, that meant I'd lost the entire frame. My dad was a welder, so the hitch was solid, and as long as the camper held, I'd have a roof over my head for the upcoming river season.

Training was grueling, but I had a lot of fun learning. It was the final days of our schooling and rookies were being chosen to go out with clients to qualify for our Class III whitewater certification.

I had done well in the class, and was anxious about my turn. I was sure a few kayakers would go first, and I was hoping to get the scoop from them about how it all went down. I wanted to be as prepared as possible when my turn came. I was also hoping I'd be picked a little bit further down the line, because the river was supposed to come up, with higher forecasted water levels making the flatwater sections a little easier to navigate. I wasn't sure how hard the guides would be judging us, and I knew I wanted to have clean lines through all of the sections, especially through the sharky flatwater, which liked to hang up boats.

A tall lanky kayaker kid was chosen first. He was experienced in his hard boat, but not in a raft. He knew how to read whitewater and had been one of the stars of the class.

We all waited anxiously for him to return from his trip, as we were sure he'd knock it outta the ballpark. He came back from his run looking deflated and grim. He unrigged his raft with his head hung low, then disappeared into his tent before any of us could ask him how it went.

Later that night, we found out that he hadn't passed. The next morning, we arrived at the boathouse, super bummed for our comrade, and even more stressed out about our turn. The river was still low and it was turning out to be a slow day.

A couple of older gentlemen walked into the shop, hoping to catch a last-minute trip down Brown's Canyon, the section of river we were doing our qualifying run on. Our rookie ears perked up as the head boatman came into the boathouse.

"Jess, you're up," the boss said.

I was freaked, not expecting to be picked second. But I had no time to panic. I got up from the boathouse lounge and started pumping up a 14-foot Avon. It was my favorite whip in the stack because it handled best in the current and took a pretty good beating in the big stuff. I grabbed some paddles and some large custy PFD's, then headed down to the beach to greet my clients and give them a quick safety talk.

I pushed off the shore, having no idea what I had just said to them, but I recalled using my fingers to count off all the points that needed to be covered in the chat. Turns out *safety third* is something we leave out with the customers, and I made sure not to mention it.

I felt super nervous, and my sunglasses were fogging up from the blush on my cheeks. I was in complete fight-or-flight mode, and I was having trouble taking in full breaths. I bumped my way down the bony flatwater section and ended up getting stuck on a rock or two. I tugged and I pulled and I got the clients to move to one side. We slid off the rocks and continued to meander down the jagged rocky stretch.

It took me a minute or two to collect myself, but then I noticed a mama Merganser and her flock of chicks, their slick mohawks glistening in the evening light as they came paddling by.

"Quack, quack, quack," they squawked as we shuffled past, perturbed that we were disrupting their evening feeding session.

They were showing off their perfect upstream ferries, and I commented on how they'd become my teachers those past few weeks as we learned how to read the river, using ferry angles to maneuver about.

I pointed out a Great Blue Heron and shared with the clients that guides abbreviate the bird by calling them GBH's for short. As I jabbered on, I found the bird's stoicism becoming a beacon of calm and clarity to my shaky nerves.

I stammered on about this and that until the pointless chatter began to bring me back to why I was there in the first place.

To be in nature and away from the hustle and bustle, flowing and free. I did my best to focus on the river, and once we entered the canyon, I began to find my flow. We coursed through the rapids and I had to do a couple spin-to-win moves through some of the rockier sections to maintain my line.

It wasn't perfect, but everyone managed to stay in the boat.

I got back to my Shasta after I was done unrigging my boat, and felt completely mortified. I didn't want to talk to anyone. I was sure I had failed my check-out run.

There's no way I passed. What was I even talking about the whole time? I got stuck on two rocks before we even got to the rapids, and I just spun the boat in circles all the way through a few of the rapids.

My father's words began to echo in my head. *I am such an idiot. Who do you think you are? You're not good enough to be a guide. What are you even doing here?*

The whole event was so upsetting, I began sobbing tears of shame and embarrassment into my pillow. I wept out loud, wishing I'd never tried out for the job in the first place.

Who did I think I was? What was I even thinking? That I'd be good enough to be a guide on the river? I'm such an idiot.

I was in complete meltdown mode when the boatman who had been my qualifying guide on our run came by my camper.

"Knock, knock," he said as he gently tapped on my door.

I hesitated, not wanting to answer, but my lights were on and my truck was parked outside, so there was no hiding from the truth that was about to hit me in the face.

I was convinced that he was going to tell me I failed, and that I was a disgrace to the company.

I was already figuring out how I could pull my camper outta there in the dark of night without any of the other rookies seeing me fleeing the scene with my tail in between my legs.

The boatman had a warm smile on his face. "You passed!" he said. "You're the first one in your class! Your name is on the board to take trips down the river tomorrow. Congratulations!"

"*What*?!" I was floored.

"I don't understand. I got stuck on a bunch of rocks, and don't you remember I just spun through Pinball and Toilet Bowl Rapids? What do you mean I passed?"

I was in complete shock.

The guide explained to me that the river will do what it does. He told me I kept my cool when things didn't go as planned and then explained that the river can be very humbling. He said that our clients had a good time and that I kept them safe and that's all that really mattered. He said he was excited to have me on the roster and wished me luck on my first season as a river runner.

I'd never felt more relieved or more empowered than I did at that moment. It was more satisfying than any piece of paper or a walk across any stage.

I had succeeded. I had graduated. I had passed my Class III whitewater rafting certification. It was like a rite of passage. It felt validating. Like I really belonged in the mountains. I felt like I finally had a home.

SINK OR SWIM

The river granted me wings. Butterfly wings. Rookie wings. I was certified to take commercial trips down the river and the autonomy of it lifted me up and gave me rise. I was taking trips down the river during the day, then driving a half an hour to Salida, slinging drinks at a local bar for some extra cash at night.

I was making some new friends who were scheming a post-Ark season adventure back East. The idea was to catch the dam release on the Gauley River, in West Virginia, then hit up a sportier section of river just north on the Youghiogheny, in Maryland.

It was the perfect solution to extend the river season, and felt like a great way to kill some time before the snow began to fly. I decided to travel back to Buffalo for a quick visit with my family before heading south to go boating.

It was getting harder and harder to go home. The cocaine scene that had already existed in Buffalo was getting hit hard with casualties from Fentanyl, and the deadly combination was plaguing the streets of Western New York. The epidemic had recently taken a few of my high school friends, and I had been home numerous times over the past few years, burying friends in the large cemetery that bordered the neighborhood I grew up in.

While I was back home, I realized that my little brother Kevin was hanging out with a really bad crowd. Kevin was only three years younger than me and had just graduated from high school. Out of fear and protection, and because I was beginning to lose childhood friends regularly to overdose, I persuaded him to come try out for the raft guide gig that following spring. All he had to do was wrap things up in Buffalo, I told him. I would figure out the rest. It was good timing because he was about to come into some money, from an insurance payout from a long-ago accident that would basically finance his trip.

As the time drew closer for Kevin to move out to Colorado, I began to have some serious reservations. The mountains had been so empowering for me, and I was trying to stay optimistic that the same opportunities the mountains had offered me, would open similar doors for him. I was determined to steer him in a new direction, but I was already feeling some serious trepidation.

As with most siblings, our relationship was complicated. We both had endured a childhood of verbal and emotional abuse, but unlike me, my brother had also dealt with the belt. As a child he had a hard time making friends, where I was quick to win them over. His boisterous character often overwhelmed me, but certain audiences appreciated his humor. He was smart and clever and always underestimated, and I just wanted to see him break out and start living his life to his highest potential.

Growing up under the same roof, we'd survived similar adversities, but the complexities of abuse can be astonishing. The shame and insecurities that burdened me weren't the same as his, and we both handled our shadows in much different ways.

I often took his shortcomings personally, and always felt a deep responsibility to protect him. I knew that this transition wasn't going to be easy for either one of us, but I was willing to give it an honest try.

Kevin suffered from a severe case of ADHD, which I believe was exacerbated by the abuse he suffered. He was put on Ritalin when we were young so that he would behave in the classroom. He took his tests in a resource room, which resembled an indoor jungle gym. He would ace his spelling tests if he was swinging from a rope, calling out the letters on his spelling list. But he failed miserably if he had to take the same test sitting at a desk with a pencil in his hand.

The ADHD affected his circadian rhythm, and he would stay up all night long, putting together K'nex or Lego sets, while the rest of us slept. One day after school, my father came home from work with a brand new VCR. It was a pretty big deal, because money was tight in our house. The VCR was set up for one day before Kevin got his hands on it. He spent the entire night taking it apart, trying to figure out how it worked.

Judging by the creations he made by moonlight, he was absolutely a bright star, but that didn't mean that he knew what was right. More often than not, his curiosity got the best of him and his actions usually ended with him getting the belt.

My mom's oldest sister was Kevin's godmother. My aunt always did her best to nurture him. When Kevin was twelve years old, she sent him to a basketball camp, which was being held at an old Franciscan college. He was running from one building to the next when he tripped over his shoelaces and fell arms first into a plate-glass door.

The door broke into large shards of glass that sliced his arms open, severing numerous nerves. He was paralyzed for almost three years from the injuries he sustained.

Kevin and my mom were constantly going back and forth to doctor's appointments and physical therapy sessions. It was a total mess and put a huge strain on our already stressful home life.

He regained most use of both of his hands and arms, but he suffered from debilitating arthritis. There was a long, drawn-out court case, rendering payouts to cover the costs of the medical bills and injuries incurred.

When the court case came to a close, my mom made sure the insurance checks were spread out over the course of many years, so that Kevin wouldn't blow all the money on hookers and blow. Literally. It was a valid concern coming from our neck of the woods.

Kevin would be receiving his first payout from the insurance claim that spring, which further prompted my persuasion to get him out of Buffalo and into the mountains. I wanted to offer him a fresh start and a new perspective on life. I felt it was the perfect time to do it.

As predicted, it was a rough start for both of us. I had pulled some strings with a friend who owned a local raft company and got Kevin on the spring training roster. I knew he wouldn't do that great if they interviewed him over the phone, so I vouched for his character.

I did this knowingly, because I was afraid he'd blow his chances of success before he even left Buffalo. I knew I was kind of sandbagging my friend, but I just wanted to get my brother out of Buffalo, and into a new scene.

With the best of intentions, I took him to get outfitted at the local kayak shop and got him suited up with all the latest gear, so he'd be prepared for his first big day on the river.

Even with all the right equipment, he still struggled to find his way. He was making enemies quicker than he was making friends, and his deep-rooted insecurities and complexes were getting the better of him. I was getting reports from some of my friends who were training the rookies that my brother was acting like a know-it-all, and was dismissive and cavalier on the river.

I came down to the boathouse to see how things were going only to find that he had completely trashed my Shasta camper, along with the land that it was sitting on. No matter what I did, or how hard I tried to make the transition easy for him, he still grappled with defeat. My heart broke each time I received a negative report from one of my new friends. I just wanted him to succeed.

I was too young and immature to handle the situation in a nurturing way. And he was too insecure and defensive to see the situation for what it was. In the end, I knew, either he had to go, or I did.

I was already feeling apprehensive about working on the river another season. The money wasn't great, and I still had to bartend to stay afloat. I had saved up enough money to move into an apartment, above an art gallery on Main Street in Salida, so I could give Kevin my Shasta when he arrived.

I'd gotten word from an inside source that the rafting company had no intentions of hiring Kevin on for the summer, and the news broke my heart.

He couldn't go back to Buffalo. There was nothing good for him there. He had restaurant experience, so I lined him up with a back-of-the-house gig at the restaurant I was bartending at. I knew the crew back there, and he would fit right in.

Next, I decided to give him my apartment, around the corner from the restaurant. He'd be all set. I had it all figured out. Or did I?

I was twenty-four years old and I had lived in Colorado for five years. In that time I had moved from Boulder to Durango to Denver, then back to Boulder, and then to Salida.

I had gotten my bachelor's degree to satisfy my mother, as it was an agreement I made with her when I decided to leave Buffalo. After graduation I had no real plan. The river seemed like a good idea. Moving my brother to Colorado seemed like a good idea. But the idea of living in the same town as my brother was clearly a bad idea.

Salida was too small a town for both of us. I had some serious guilt about leaving him there alone, but I was at a loss for how I could advocate for him any longer. I was positive my mom would be upset with me for abandoning him in a new town, but her disapproval didn't stop me.

Valerie had been living in Telluride since our stint in Denver, and she said the restaurant she worked at would be hiring. So I packed up my truck with everything I owned, and headed to the San Juans. The guilt ate at me, but the decision was made. I was headed to Telluride to start over once again.

CHAPTER

3

DAY TWO: JUNE 11TH, 2021

Your children are not your children.
They are sons and daughters of Life's longing for itself.
They come through you but not from you.
And though they are with you yet they belong not to you.
You may give them your love but not your thoughts,
For they have their own thoughts.
You may house their bodies but not their souls,
For their souls dwell in the house of tomorrow,
which you cannot visit, not even in your dreams.
You may strive to be like them, but seek not to make them like you.
For life goes not backward nor tarries with yesterday.
You are the bows from which your children as living arrows are sent forth.
The archer sees the mark upon the path of the infinite, and He bends you with
His might that His arrows may go swift and far.
Let your bending in the archer's hand be for gladness.
For even as He loves the arrow that flies,
so He also loves the bow that is stable."

— Kahlil Gibran

PAPA'S MAP

The winds finally died down as Chason navigated the flows. Putt-putt on the motor and puff-puff on the spliff, we traveled the still current until we became unsure of whether we were ascending or descending the river. The sleeping river isle seemed to not be moving a single mile. Chason tied up our rig to a river shore tammy, and we slept on our boat, under the stars, until the red dawn awoke.

The morning mood was dreamy. Almost as if we were floating through the mists of Avalon, about to embark into a whole new realm. We both awoke damp with morning dew, and after Chason caressed me with some butterfly kisses with his eyelashes he felt obliged to get back behind the motor. Him on the throttle, and me on my Paco pad, he steered us down the still, muddy waters. We made our way down, doing our best not to arouse the Great Blue Heron, who stood silent and proud. Like a statue, he let us pass by, stoic in his knowing, astute and wise, in wild wonder. Did he know what lay ahead?

It was a quiet morning, and we were both entranced by its brilliant light. The sky reflected a deep crimson red, as if mirroring the ancient rock of the Paradox Formation. As morning turned to day, the towering burnt clay castles began to rise. Our borrowed bimini bore the only witness to our newlywed bodies, its shade saving our first hours of wedlock, protecting us from the relentless sun. Nothing to do but make love and chase shadows.

I couldn't help but think to myself how lucky I was. Chason Russell was a born legend. He had traveled to the world's depths searching for adventure. Never for the accolades. Only for the experience. All the while staying humble and curious.

While Chason steered, I looked over the river map his father Papa had given us just before we hit the road.

"Here ya go," Papa said. "I've got some good notes in there for ya." It was a sweet gesture from the stoic man.

As I read the map, I noticed a note with Papa's handwriting that said, "Mile Marker 13. Chason Hits Rock - 1996."

I laughed out loud, then shared the mention with him. He tilted his head back, then laughed. "Yeah, I remember hitting that rock," shaking his head at the memory.

Much like life—and much like this story—our journey down the Colorado River was not linear. We consciously chose to leave our books and journals at home. We kept our watches in the car and made a point to only use our phones when we wanted to capture the moments most meaningful to us. We did not want to feel the constraints of time as we floated the lazy river miles.

Our voyage was not going to be marked by mile markers. They meant nothing to us on this trip. Chason and I were blissfully riding the river's goldilocks flows, one power stroke at a time. We allowed the sun to decide where we ate and where we slept. We used our motor to ascend and descend the river as we saw fit, sometimes having dinner on one side of the river only to pack up our kitchen and camp on some other nearby beach.

Goldilocks, who constantly struggled to find her way, was one of our many inside jokes. Chason, the extreme adventurer, and me, the reserved comrade in-tow, we often had to find a common middle ground when navigating life together. Don't get me wrong, I love Type 2 adventuring. *You know, the kind of adventuring where it's only fun in hindsight.* But my fun-to-fear ratio was a bit more reeled-in compared to Chason's risk-tolerant nature. Chason made a point of chasing the Goldilocks flows when he planned our adventures together. Nothing too scary, but just scary enough to make it feel like we were on a real adventure. *Soft adventures*, he liked to jest. *Soft Adventures with Chason and Jess.*

*****

LAS MONTAÑAS

I was lost in thought, feeling guilty for leaving Kevin behind in Salida, but excited for the road that lay ahead. Telluride is breathtaking the first time you lay eyes on her. While driving in, I fixated on a thin white strip pouring out of the face of the mountain. I wondered whether it was a vein of snow leftover from the winter season or a cascading waterfall, perfectly placed at the center of the idyllic mountain town.

Just as I was realizing the white strip was a waterfall, I found myself slamming into a huge speed bump strategically placed at the end of the spur, letting me know I'd made it into town. It seemed symbolic. *Just another bump in the road.*

Rolling into Telluride the summer of 2006, I was floored by its beauty. I had skied there a few times before, but the peaks were always hidden under storm clouds, and I had never really seen just how beautiful the place really was. The mountains were so impressive and the waterfall that had captured my attention was so awe-inspiring it left me feeling sanguine and hopeful. The spires and cliffs that buttressed the tiny town only added to the charm of the old Victorians that lined the main drag. I felt like I had landed in Switzerland, worlds away from the troubles I'd left behind in Salida.

It was still the age of no cell phones so I had no way of reaching Valerie when I got there. I rolled down Main Street, parked my rig, then started walking around, looking for a restaurant called Las Montañas where Val was scheduled to work later on that day.

The restaurant was smack-dab in the middle of it all, just like the mountains that towered over me. There were no customers inside, but the door was wide open and Manu Chao was blasting over the speakers while clips of kayaking gnar played on TV screens. I grabbed a stool and bellied up to the bar.

A guy walked out from the kitchen. He asked if he could help me and I told him I was looking for my best friend Valerie. He said he didn't know where she was, but that she was scheduled to work a little later. Then he offered me a drink.

We got to chatting and I discovered that his name was Y.B. I had a feeling he was the owner, as Valerie had told me all about him. After a few minutes of small talk, we realized that we had both just gotten off the Roaring Fork River in Aspen—kayaking and, in my case, R2'ing a stretch of river called Slaughterhouse. It turned out that we both had worked on the Arkansas, him in Canon City, me in Buena Vista. He said he was the head boatman for a company called Buff Joe's, an infamous outfit that had a hilarious bumper sticker boasting "I Heart B.J.'s"

We shared a couple funny stories about working on the Ark, then I asked him what YB stood for. He said there was an old river guide that worked at Buff Joe's whose name was Brad, and that the boaters started calling the old guy OB, for Old Brad, and started calling him YB for Young Brad.

His story got cut short when a girl walked in, ready to start her shift. I told her I was looking for Valerie, then she pointed me in the right direction. I thanked YB for the drink, then took off looking for my gal pal Val.

When I finally found her, I immediately felt reassured. I told her I needed to find work ASAP, and she told me that Las Montañas was hiring. I put together a resume and gave it to my new friend YB and he put me on the schedule. I was off to a fresh start.

I made a new friend named Tanya who cocktailed on Friday nights, the same night I was scheduled to bartend. She was well connected in the community, and I could tell she knew how to have a good time. She was a super feisty Italian girl from Flint, Michigan, and we bonded while bitching over rude tables and shitty tippers. I was immediately drawn to her sassy Rust Belt attitude. I felt like we shared a camaraderie having grown up in similar suburbs of blue-collar cities.

She had just started kayaking and was super down to go boating, whenever. After leaving my rafting community behind, I decided I should probably figure out how to kayak, since I didn't have a boathouse full of rafts to pull from anymore. I knew how to read the river, and Tanya knew how to roll her kayak. Theoretically, all I needed to do was learn how to roll my kayak and we'd be good to go.

Tanya and YB became my new kayak friends, our free time consumed with roll sessions at the local hot springs and chasing winter runoff in the spring. I was building a community and I could feel a shift in my trajectory. The river was coursing my life into a new direction, and I was ready for the current to take me away.

THE OBSERVATORY

Back in Boulder, when I first moved to Colorado, my roommate Buck took me up to ski Vail Resort for my first real powder day. As we unloaded the lift, off he went in a powder puff of glitter, the last I saw of him for the afternoon. "No friends on a powder day!" he called, not even looking back.

Buck was born and bred in Telluride, a real mountain kid. I had never heard of "Taaalluride" before moving to Colorado, and often got picked on while trying to pronounce the town's name with my thick Buffalo accent.

On our way home from skiing that day, Buck told me a story about a place called the Alta Lakes Observatory, a backcountry hut built by his friend Chason Russell's father where he and his friends would hang out, ski, and party. I remember a sparkle in his eyes as he reminisced about the place. I felt equally mystified and intrigued by the way Buck told stories of his dear friend, Chason Russell. His childhood seemed so different from mine, and I remember hoping I'd find myself there one day, to take it all in.

I pictured a castle more than a hut, surrounded by towering peaks, and a landscape bombarded by pillowy powder fields. I imagined the sky so close, that the milky way would swim like a sea of stars, silky smooth and close to the touch. I envisioned a constellation room, housing a large telescope, that offered a closer look into the galaxies that circled above.

As I would later see for myself, the Alta Lakes Observatory is nestled in the thick pine forest of the San Juan Mountains. The rugged landscape is backlit by craggily couloirs, littered with abandoned mining fields and adorned with crystal-clear high alpine lakes. It is a place hospitable only to mountain lions, bears, elk, and the occasional alpinist.

The ambiance of the place emanates the aesthetic of an era long forgotten, with a red phone booth that could very well have been a portal for time travel and a pick-up truck that could very well have transported moonshine during the days of prohibition. A mine trestle sits perched high above, and in winter positions itself as a perfect ramp for any ski enthusiast to creatively express their gratitude for the champagne powder that blankets the landing below.

Built with sweat and grit, it's a true example of fortitude in the high country. The family who built the Observatory, the Russells, may be just as famous as the hut itself. Jim Russell—the man I would later come to call, as everyone did, Papa—began its construction in 1975, when the Telluride Ski Area was first being built.

I got my first invite to the Observatory that first winter I lived in Telluride. I was dating a guy named Andy, whom I met while I was bartending at Las Montañas, when a group of us were planning a river adventure. I quickly fell in love with his boyish good looks and Eagle Scout ways. It was an added bonus when I found out that he was a really good skier and liked to paddle Class IV.

I had just gotten a fresh pair of Volkl Gotamas mounted with a pair of Fritschi alpine touring bindings. They were my first pair of real backcountry skis, and I was so psyched to use them to ski into the hut. Properly equipped, I approached the ridge of Prospect Bowl on the Telluride Ski Area with Andy. We ducked a boundary rope and skied into Gold King Basin where the infamous hut was perched. My inner rebel was thrilled. I was really doing it. I was skiing into the Observatory.

The slope's west-facing aspect meant that the snow surface had melted and then frozen into a hard crust, but before I knew it, I found myself some fresh snow just in time to face-plant into a tree well. I untangled my skis, then lifted myself out of the piney scrub and sun-eaten snow. After a quick head-to-toe assessment, we both deemed myself okay, then I fumbled my way to the hut.

The party was just beginning. Libations were consumed and mushroom caps were being taken. As the moon began to rise, a bunch of us geared up and headed out on a mini ski tour towards a low-angle powder field. Under a blanket of stars someone warned, "Better put on your moonscreen!" as tiny powder flakes glistened under the moon's big bright light.

The skin track was manageable, and I felt empowered by my abilities to keep up with the group. I made a new girlfriend at the top of our first lap. We introduced ourselves, and she said that her friends called her Mama Bear, which I felt was fitting. I could tell the Telluride locals held her in high regard and I was super stoked to meet another female in the backcountry.

I also met the legendary Chason Russell that night. He was shy and soft spoken, with a cool and calm that was noticeably charming in an awkward, but confident, knows-his-shit kind of way. He had just moved back to Telluride after graduating with a degree in photography at Montana State University. He was back in the San Juans working for an education program called the Telluride Academy, which takes kids on all kinds of outdoor adventures. I was always a little jealous of the activities posted on the library bulletin board, secretly wishing I'd had those same opportunities when I was a kid.

Chason was pretty mysterious, and I was pretty psyched to get a minute to connect with him. After we were introduced, I asked him how he'd gotten his name. I was a little shocked at how forward I was, but I relaxed as soon as he began to tell me.

With an air of esteem he explained. "It was inspired by my grandfather's name Charles, on my mother's side, and the winter constellation Orion, which lies high in the sky just above Ajax Mountain in the winter."

I thought, "Ok, I'm not even remotely cool enough to be talking to this guy!" But he just kept chatting me up, and his welcoming attitude made me feel like I belonged in this amazing mountain community.

THE ACADEMY

Over the years Chason became a friend while we adventured in the mountains together. As time went by I became more and more in awe of his skills and abilities. As our friendship grew, I realized that Chason was not only an amazingly talented mountain man, but also an incredible ambassador of the outdoors. He approached the backcountry with graceful consideration and admirable respect. He always had so much to teach and so much wisdom to offer.

Chason Patrick Russell was born under Piscenian skies, on March 10th, 1980. Born and raised in the San Juan Mountains, his childhood was anything but ordinary. Instead of your typical playground and mat time experience, Chason began attending the Telluride Academy in the summer months, when school was out of session. Coincidentally, the academy was established in 1980, the same year Chason was born, to provide opportunities and child care for Telluride's working class families.

Chason's parents both had to work full time jobs in order to build their lives in the mountains. Salli, Chason's mother, was a chef for the private-jet owners who flew in and out of Telluride, and his father Papa owned and operated the New Sheridan Old Bar. Chason and his younger brother, Garrett, attended every week of the academy, never missing a single camping trip, river excursion, climbing ascent or hiking exploration in those impressionable younger days.

It was no wonder that, as Chason got older, he ended up skiing the biggest mountain lines and paddling the coldest winter run-off. Chason wasn't just surrounded by dramatic and moody 14,000-foot peaks. They made up the very fabric of his soul.

Influenced by his camp counselors, Chason quickly learned how to navigate the world in a unique and resourceful way. Pam East, one of his closest camp counselors, bonded quickly with Chason when he was just six years old. In those early years the Academy was still in its infancy. Pam mostly took the kids to the playground in Town Park, to the soccer fields to kick some balls around, or to the river to skip rocks. They'd eat ice cream cones on their way back to the Academy School House.

One of the key pillars of the Academy is inclusivity. Its founder, Wendy Brooks—a beloved woman who died in 2024, at age 84—honed in on the importance of this moral from the program's very inception. She wanted to make it clear that the academy was not just for the children of Telluride, but for anyone who wanted to engage with the outdoors. Many of the Academy camps were filled with city kids and country kids from all over the United States. Chason became the poster child of this inclusivity, welcoming all who came to explore his backyard.

In the late eighties, Wendy changed the format of the Academy from a daycare setting to more of a day camp platform. Pam began planning adventurous programs that included rock climbing, river running, and backpacking. The Telluride kids were sprouting, so the Academy needed to grow with them. The Telluride Public School jumped on board and began offering a scholarship program to cover the costs for students who needed financial assistance to attend the summer academia. Chason was awarded a full scholarship.

It wasn't long before he became a consultant to Pam, offering advice on what adventures they should do next. Chason was becoming skilled at reading maps, planning itineraries and shuttles, meal prepping, and organizing all the proper equipment for multi-sport expeditions. At the ripe age of eleven, Chason began going on trips with kids from out of town three to four years his senior. The kids never gave him a hard time for being younger, but rather looked up to him for his knowledge and experience in the mountains.

When Chason was 15, he became a junior camp counselor. Because he wasn't 18 yet, he had to keep his trips local. Chason planned his trips all around the San Juan Mountains, and especially loved to plan excursions where he and his group would walk out the back door of the Academy and end up in nearby towns like Silverton and Ouray, showing kids from all over the world how to travel through and respect the mountains.

CHASING PHOTOS

When Chason's father Papa had free time, he would take Chason and Garrett down the backyard rivers in their family raft, teaching them how to row and navigate the current. Chason was not a strong swimmer and he never felt completely comfortable in a raft. He said the big rubber raft made him feel too exposed to the whitewater.

When Chason was about eight, Bill Glasscock, a Telluride Academy counselor and close family friend, brought over a kayak for him to try. The boat was way too big, but Bill threw some padding in the cockpit to secure Chason's hips, then took him down to the Moab Daily section on the Colorado River. It took Chason about 30 minutes to figure out his roll, and then they were off. Bill showed Chason how to paddle in and out of eddies, and to his amazement, Chason took to the sport like a fish takes to water.

The oversized kayak became an extension of Chason's body, and at the ripe age of eight he became Bill's protege, running classic San Juan backyard runs on the Dolores and the Lower San Miguel rivers. Bill would come to Chason's house on school days, picking him up to go paddle. Salli would come to the front door, yelling with a wink, "This is school PE, right, Bill?"

When Chason was about 12 years old, Bill found a size-appropriate kayak for Chason to paddle: a white Perception, a classic river running hard boat of its time, that fit him perfectly. Bill saw it was time for Chason to up his kayaking game, and he began taking him down the Ledges section on the Lower San Miguel. They would camp and surf and paddle through the moonlight, chasing the sparkle that only the midnight hours can provide.

When Chason was 16, he and Bill began taking bigger adventures together. Once, while driving over Ophir Pass to paddle the Upper Animas River, a classic class IV-V run, Chason made Bill stop just as they were cresting the top of the pass. Bill was driving an old blue '82 Datsun pickup with four kayaks strapped to the top.

"Stop the truck!" Chason shouted.

He hopped out of the Datsun and reached into one of his dry bags for his camera. After he found it, he ran out a few yards in front of the pick-up and pointed his camera at the truck.

"Alright Bill, drive real slow, I'm gonna start taking some action shots, while you drive along this wall of snow right there!"

The scene couldn't have been more picturesque. North Lookout consumed the backdrop, while 15-foot walls of snow cut through the road, perfectly framing the shot. The beat-up Datsun was adorned with four brightly colored kayaks strapped on top, with Bill hanging out the window. It was a classic shot, and Chason developed the photo in his dark room at school, then submitted it to a few headliner magazines, hoping to get published.

A few weeks later, Chason showed up at Bill's house in a fit.

Chason banged on Bill's door, then let himself in. "Hey Bill, where are you? *Bill*!" Chason yelled as he made his way through the old miner's cabin.

Bill burst out of his bedroom, boasting a smile. Hearing the excitement in Chason's voice he asked, "Hey man! What's up?! What's going on?"

Chason waved an envelope in Bill's direction.

"Bill, you won't believe it! I sent that photo of you on the Ophir Pass over to *National Geographic* and they want to publish it in their next edition. They sent me a check, and I want to give you ten percent of my earnings."

This was way before social media, and way before digital photos, a time when cameras still took film and many photographers still developed their own photos.

"Hey man, no worries! You keep that money! You earned that check!" Bill said. He was not about to take Chason's hard-earned commission. He was just happy to have been his muse for the inspirational shot. After earning that first check, adventure photography quickly became Chason's passion.

CHASING BIG MOUNTAINS

When school was in session, Chason left the Academy world and entered into the ski club scene, as one of the rising stars on the Bump Club, Telluride's mogul team. Brian O'Neill was Chason's coach and the two of them skied more than just bumps together. Back in the early nineties, Telluride had nine lifts. The upper terrain open today was still considered backcountry, and you had to hike it to earn your turns.

Dynamo, a famous run off the top of Gold Hill Bowl, was a stout hike from the top of Chair Six. On a classic powder day when Chason was ten, Brian thought he'd show him some more advanced terrain on Gold Hill Bowl.

Brian broke trail as the two booted up to the top. As they looked down the pristine powder run, Chason took no time at all to just point his skis downhill, charging down the mountain. Dynamo is a big wide open bowl up top, but then chokes down to a narrow couloir for about 30 feet in length, that then opens up again into a beautifully pitched apron.

The two skied their way down the steep and deep terrain, then made their way through the narrow choke that gives Dynamo the feel of an hourglass.

When they got to the bottom Chason asked if they could go for another. Then another. And another. On their fourth hike back up, Brian was just about to reach the headwall when he looked behind him and saw Chason crawling up the booter, barely hanging on. Brian thought to himself, "Oh my God, what have I done to this kid?" In a panic he started making his way back down to Chason.

When he got to him, Chason just looked at him and said, "Go. Go! We gotta go! These guys behind me are catching up!" That's when Brian knew he had created a true powder-hound.

When Chason was 14, Brian started taking him out on bigger ski adventures. The San Joaquin Couloir is an iconic line that can be approached from either skiing and skinning out the backcountry gate off Telluride Ski Area or from the Ophir town side. Back in those days, if you wanted to approach a big line like the San Joaquin, you had to ski on telemark skis, their free-heel bindings allowing for you to walk with the skis still strapped to your feet. Chason was mostly an alpine skier, but once given the opportunity to join some of the most prestigious skiers in town on their backcountry adventures, he traded in his alpine skis for teles.

Brian, Chason, and two other men decided to approach the couloir from the Ophir side. As they made their way up the mostly south, south-east-facing 4,000-foot ascent, Brian could tell that Chason would be a promising ski alpinist. He had no problem keeping up with his senior counterparts and even outshined them when they entered the couloir and found that the crux move, a tight choke halfway down, was an un-edgeable icy skating rink.

The other two guys decided to put their skis on their backpacks and down-climb the feature. After watching them struggle their way through the solid ice without crampons, Brian decided to straight line the feature, hoping to clear the ice. He instructed Chason to do the same, and positioned himself below Chason in case anything went wrong. At least he could catch him if he caught an edge.

"Alright Chason, just ski it how I skied it, then safety right here, next to us," Brian shouted with hesitation in his voice. Again, Brian began questioning himself: *What have I done to this kid?*

"Alright. Dropping!" Chason shouted back, no fear in his tone.

As if he'd done it a million times, Chason made one jump turn, pointed his skis down hill, then bunny-hopped as if levitating off the snow. He straightlined the entire icy choke in one smooth move, then buttered a wind feature that had accumulated at the bottom of the choke before smoothly stopping just below the other men. Chason wasn't just tagging along with these local legends. He was showing them how it was done.

By that point, Chason was no longer interested in skiing for Bumps Club. He had his eyes on a bigger prize. He wanted to ski the big mountain terrain he had grown up hiking in the summer months while attending the Academy, and he wanted to photograph his adventures while doing it. Brian was roommates with a professional ski photographer named Thomas Robert Youngstrom.

T.R. was a legend when it came to photographing skiers in some of the most remote and exotic places around the globe. Chason was enamored with T.R. and everything that he stood for. Travel, skiing big-lines, and capturing the spirit of the sport. T.R. took to Chasons humble demeanor and began mentoring him in the world of photography and backcountry skiing.

In 1995 extreme skiing was becoming more mainstream and Brian and T.R. were pushing the limits in the San Juans Mountains. They had their eyes on Rollings Mountain, a rugged 13,000-foot peak that is seldom summited in summer, let alone skied when it's covered in snow in the middle of the unpredictable winter.

It is a chossy mountain that can be accessed via the East Ridge. Their intentions were to ski the west aspect. It was late winter and conditions were lining up. After a six-hour approach, Chason and the men reached the middle summit of the mountain. Google Maps and drones were not available back in those days, which made ski mountaineering even less accessible. Oftentimes, skiing off these remote peaks meant skiing them blindly, not necessarily knowing whether an entrance led to a clean line that could be skied, or one that would require a rope to rappel.

As the men made their way down the couloir, T.R. began to show Chason how to look at skiing from a different perspective. Ski photography wasn't just about skiing the line in style. It was also about setting yourself up so you could capture your ski partner making the most beautiful turn, with the perfect backdrop in the frame.

As they made their way down the steep terrain, they found themselves in a position where the snow ended and a cliff emerged. After long assessment, they decided the safest way through the choss was to launch themselves onto a ten-foot, postage stamp–sized landing, setting themselves up to weasel their way into another couloir that would lead to an open apron.

Brian went first. He could see that it was a technical move, in a for-sure no-fall zone. After making the precarious jump turn, he stood down below, again thinking to himself, "What have I gotten this kid into?" That's when he recalled what Salli had told him when he picked Chason up that morning.

"Whatever you do, don't kill my kid, Brian!" Her voice echoed in his head as he watched Chason lick the stamp. He sent the big drop, laying down his skis and styling the move, no problem.

As the three men made their way back to the car, they traversed across the frozen Trout Lake. Reflecting on the day, both Brian and T.R. found themselves thinking that it was hard to believe Chason was only fifteen years old and skiing these huge consequential lines, when he was only a sophomore in high school. They knew Chason was going to go far. Both in the sport, and around the world.

On August 9th, 1997, while Brian was attending a wedding, he received news that T.R. had died in a helicopter crash in the Chilean Andes, where he was skiing and shooting photos. Brian and Chason were crushed. And although Chason had lost his mentor to the mountains, he did not lose his drive for adventure photography.

CHASING RIVERS

The kayak crew in the San Juans was tight-knit, and there was a great sense of trust that enabled them to push the boundaries of kayaking. In the late 90s and early 2000s Chason began paddling with Russell Kelly, a Telluride boater who was expedition kayaking when nobody else in their right mind was. Russell's approach to paddling took Chason's kayaking to an entirely new level. If Russell would go, Chason would go.

The river opened Chason up to a new community of love, loss, and support. Annie Quathamer, Russell Kelly's girlfriend, was just getting into paddling, but in August of 2004, shortly after they started dating, Russell died in a car crash. The loss shook the entire boating community. A few years after his untimely death, Annie began dating another strong class V kayaker named Damon Miller. But Damon, too, died tragically—in a motorcycle accident on his way home from a trip to Mexico in August 2006.

The river was dangerous. That was part of the allure. But curiously, the crew was losing its most influential mentors to the road, not the rapids. As the community encountered profound grief, they found refuge from the pain in one another. Chason's compassionate and gentle nature, in particular, helped Annie paddle through her grief.

In a male-dominated sport, Chason became Annie's new mentor. Over the years, the two friends paddled all over Colorado, and as far as Peru and India. When she paddled with Chason, he lifted her up and continually encouraged her.

In 2007, Chason and Annie traveled to Nepal to paddle the remote Marsyangdi River. Marasyandi literally means raging river, and Chason had faith and confidence that he and Annie were capable of paddling it. Due to its gradient, it was a world-class destination—a free-flowing river that has since been dammed. Since Annie and Chason kayaked it, three hydro projects have made paddling the Marsyangdi River a thing of the past.

After their trip to Nepal, the two of them began a kayaking program through the Telluride Academy. Together they planned a trip down the Crystal River drainage just outside of Aspen. Chason had been wanting to bring the Academy kids to that part of the state for a long time. He knew that the Elk Mountains served as an incredible watershed offering all levels of paddling, from easy class II to rowdy class V whitewater, and he was excited to open the kids' eyes to some different river systems.

To be safe, Chason demonstrated to the young and impressionable paddlers how to run the meaty Class V section of whitewater on the Crystal River called Meat Grinder, while Annie and the students watched from the banks. After he safely made his way through the Class V rapid, Annie led the more advanced paddlers down the Narrows section, a stout Class IV section of whitewater just downstream.

The Narrows is still an advanced run, but only the most experienced kayakers run the Meat Grinder. It was way too dangerous to take the students down this section of whitewater. Annie and the kids watched in amazement as Chason ran the upper Meat Grinder section in awe. He paddled with such intention and focus, it was inspiring for the children to see just what was possible if they continued to paddle hard in the sport.

DAY THREE: JUNE 12TH, 2021

Where to from here?
Away from the hustle and bustle
Captivating creativity
Free flowing and free
Where to from here?
Deep dark precipice
Filled with fear and unknown
Drowned by the darkness
Heavy with looming shadows
For there is light
White as a snowflake
Culmination of creativity
A drifting current on a collision course
With Destiny

—Chason Russell

RAVEN'S RECKONING

I often joked that Chason loved to have his cake and eat it too—always considering all the ways to enjoy each precious moment. True to form, Chason found us a stretch of beach where we could have some evening shade for an easy dinner. After we ate, we crossed the river and made camp in a spot where we would escape the blazing early morning sun and enjoy some much needed shade while eating breakfast.

I sat on the boat as he unloaded our minimal kitchen supplies. I looked up at the canyon walls and noticed the moon was beginning its waxing phase. A waxing gibbous crescent began to rise between two burnt red rocky castles in the sky. As I took in the scenery I noticed a lone raven that had been traveling with us since the start of our trip. The raven was circling high above in a heat thermal, rising higher and higher.

Chason fired up our little Jetboil stove and started to make us each a cup of tea. After he lit the canister, he sat down on a beached log. I watched him and began to think,

I am so lucky that this strong, capable, competent, calculated, humble man is my husband. Look at him. He will be setting up my kitchen, and he will be making me tea, and he will be my partner from here on out. I cannot wait to grow old with him. Waves of relief, safety, security, and reassurance washed over me.

From afar, I watched as Chason summoned the attention of the lone black bird. The raven swooped down, like a bomb, then gently landed in the sand and began pecking at his feet.

Ravens are known for traveling in pairs. On the river they work together as opportunists, cleverly devising plans to sneak snacks from their river patrons. We'd seen this raven each day, but always alone. *This raven must have lost its partner,* I thought to myself.

My sweet feelings of relief were quickly rinsed away with a wave of panic. Dark thoughts began to creep in.

What if I have a stroke at fifty, and Chason has to take care of me? What if I become a burden for the rest of our lives? How could I do that to him? To this man who loves nothing but

adventure? That would destroy him. I must be as healthy as I can now, so I never put him in that position later.

I was sabotaging the most meaningful moments with *what-if*'s instead of being present watching Chason and the raven, waiting for my cup of tea. I was sabotaging my joy with hereafters.

Hadn't I known better? Hadn't I already learned not to do this. Hadn't I learned to not fret about the future. To just be present. To be here now?

*****

PLEASURE PARK

It was a classic Colorado summer day in 2009. The late August sun was starting to shine low, and the sky was a deep indigo blue. That blue that looks purple silhouetted against the craggy ridges of the San Juan Mountains.

My friends and I were headed out on a backyard adventure. First, we planned to kayak the Gunnison Gorge, then backpack through the Weminuche Wilderness. It was a celebration to an ending, and a cheers to a new beginning in honor of our friend Miss Fitz, a fly fishing guide on the Gunnison River. She was leaving Colorado to pursue a degree in natural medicine in Portland, Oregon.

Miss Fitz would be guiding her last three-day commercial fly-fishing trip, and we wanted to plan a proper send-off. The timing was going to work out perfectly. A small group of us would paddle the Gunny Gorge as a day trip, catching up to Miss Fitz on her last day on the same stretch. Miss Fitz would finish up her commercial trip, then drop off her clients back at the angler shop. Then we'd all head to the trailhead to backpack for a couple nights in the wilderness.

The desert sun danced in the sky as we paddled down the gorge. We chased shade, maneuvered around boulders, rode fun wave trains, and hooted and hollered as we nailed our combat rolls.

The canyon walls echoed with giggles for miles that day, and I wondered if Miss Fitz could feel our presence in the gorge. After the rapids, there is a long stretch of flatwater before the takeout. Floating down the slow and steady rio, I found myself in deep thought.

Miss Fitz is guiding her last trip before diving into academia. She is saying good-bye to the San Juans. Headed for the big city to study Chinese herbs, acupuncture, and medicine. What an opportunity. To be engrossed in botany, pharmacology, anatomy, pathophysiology, chemistry. What a dream it would be to pursue such a powerful and challenging passion. She is so courageous to leave this lifestyle behind for the pursuit of the unknown.

I was in awe of her clarity. Of her direction. Of her confidence. Of her fortitude. I wondered if I could ever do something like that. Study something so important and so impactful. I wondered if I could commit to something that hard. Her choice to leave the mountains for the city really made an impression on me.

We reached the banks of the Pleasure Park takeout and began to load up our kayaking gear in the usual takeout chaos. "Paddles over here! Boats ready to be loaded, over there!"

I was looking for some cam-straps to secure kayaks to the roof of my truck when I heard someone's phone ring. As Tanya handed up a kayak, I looked over and saw Miss Fitz's boyfriend, Mike, on his phone. His face was pale, his jaw had dropped open, and he had a blank stare that frightened me. As I stepped down from the tire of my truck, I could feel the air suddenly get thick. Something was wrong.

As I approached Mike, I could see tears building up in the corners of his eyes.

"Is everything okay?" I asked with hesitation.

"Miss Fitz is gone," he whispered softly. "She's dead."

"*What*?! *What do you mean she's dead*? She was just on the river. How could she be dead?!"

He had gotten the call. The call where there is no going back. No going back to the life you once knew. The life you were living is over. That life is gone. Everything you knew, no matter what you do or how hard you bargain, has changed forever.

After dropping off her clients at the angler shop, Miss Fitz had headed towards town to meet us for the second part of our adventure. Another driver had turned out into traffic, right in front of the Volkswagen van she was riding shotgun in. It was a head-on collision. A collision course with destiny. She was killed instantly. We were all floored. Confused. Bewildered. In complete shock.

"Wait, what?! We are supposed to go meet her, right now, then go hike the Weminuche. What do you mean, she was killed in a car accident. She was just floating and fishing down the river, right in front of us."

And just like that, Miss Fitz was gone.

We had planned a trek in the mountains, to send off our good friend on her next adventure. Little did we know that her last adventure was down the Gunnison Gorge. There would be another kind of celebration for her departure, but it looked a lot different than the one we had anticipated.

ONLY LOVE IS REAL

Acelebration of Miss Fitz's life was planned, something that was entirely new to me. My version of a memorial included a wake, where the family of the deceased stand in a line, shaking hands and hugging strangers while guests say their last respects. That agonizing greeting line is then followed by a showing in a stuffy funeral parlor, where a stranger speaks to the legacy of the loved one who has just passed. Then everyone drives, lights flashing and funeral flags waving, to the cemetery, where we bury our loved one in a big field planted with our friends and relatives who have passed before us. There's a quick prayer at the foot of the freshly dug grave, and then a melancholy dinner with cheap beer and beef-on-weck. The whole ordeal is expensive, depressing, and sheds no light on where the dead have gone, or what anyone should do next.

Tanya, YB, Andy and I drove to the celebration of life together. It was being held at a ranch up on Wilson Mesa, just outside of Telluride. Motoring up the windy roads, overlooking the 14,000-foot peaks, I found myself trying to conceptualize the endless amounts of scree and rock that made up the mountains. My mind began to wander. I began thinking about all the people I'd lost: some to drugs, some to car accidents, some to cancer, some to suicide. All unexpected, and all before their time. I felt so sad and so disappointed. I was upset that the world would be missing out on Miss Fitz. On all of them.

Why Miss Fitz? She was going to do some much good in the world. Why her? She was going to make a positive impact. She was going to make a difference.

I was bargaining. Why her and not some low-life who wasn't doing any good. Nothing about the universe made sense to me. Death can make you feel that way. Out of control and in utter disarray.

A crowd began to amass in a meadow overlooking the Wilson Range. The gathering exuded celebration, yet the hues of the distant mountains matched the blues that everyone was feeling that day. A large circle of people had formed and there were prayer flags blowing in the wind. Miss Fitz's father, Señor Fitz, got up in front of the mourners and began to speak.

His words were full of gratitude and respect. In a soft tone, he told us that it was her time to go. He illuminated us with his deep knowledge and understanding of death. He explained that her light had shown so bright, that it was now time for us to share her light and pass it on. This was how he wanted us to honor her.

I was beyond confused. *Why wasn't he angry and upset? Why wasn't he cursing the heavens?* His ability to accept the loss of his daughter felt unnatural to me. She was not my own flesh and blood, but a new friend, and even I was struggling to wrap my head around her passing. His eulogy felt strangely insensitive, and it made me feel really uncomfortable.

Wasn't it too new? I thought. *Wasn't it too soon? Wasn't it too unorthodox to ever really find acceptance or closure. Especially when the death is so untimely and so abrupt? Wasn't the wound too raw?*

But with his words, I slowly realized, Señor Fitz was showing me a new way of grieving, and it could not have been more different than the process I was used to. Even though the whole experience made me feel uneasy, I couldn't help but feel some truth in his words. I was intrigued by his ability to make sense of death so soon.

After his speech, Tanya and I introduced ourselves to Señor Fitz. We asked how he found acceptance in his daughters passing so quickly.

He mentioned a psychiatrist, Brian Weiss, whose books had helped him earlier in his life when he was experiencing deep feelings of grief. Describing sessions with various patients, Dr. Weiss explained a deeper understanding of the soul and its experience down here on Earth. His writings covered things like reincarnation, past life regression, future life progression, and the survival of the soul after death.

I had never heard of any of these topics before. I was emotionally drained and overstimulated by the whole experience, but I couldn't help but be mystified and fascinated by everything Señor Fitz had said.

After the memorial, I purchased two books by Brian Weiss. I needed to know more. I needed to know what reincarnation really meant, and what past life regression looked like. I had always heard the word, soul, but rarely used it, especially when speaking in regard to death.

In reading them, I had an *aha* moment. First, I realized that we all have a soul. Secondly, I learned that the soul is never born and the soul never dies.

Then I realized that if we all have a soul, and that the soul is eternal, then we are all bound to meet again. This teaching resonated. It made more sense than anything I had ever been taught in the Catholic Church. When learning about the soul in Sunday school as a child, I remember the teacher speaking to the body and soul as being one. But never that the body is just a vessel for the soul. The only real take away I ever really received while going to church was to feel shame for my sins. And boy did that stay with me.

But in this new teaching of the soul, I began to have a different idea about what happened after we leave this world. And this new realization brought me hope. I began to think that perhaps after we die, there is potential that we will all meet our loved ones again. And then again and again. Samsara. The birth, death and rebirth. I later learned that this was at the core of Buddhist teachings. It was something I wanted to believe in. But I didn't exactly know how.

These new ideas brought me peace. But they also brought on more questions. I was grateful for Sr. Fitz's insight, and was able to find my first lesson and gift in Miss Fitz's passing. It was a new way to honor someone who had passed and a new way to shine light on tragedy. I was 28 years old, and up until this celebration of life, I had never explored the emotional landscape of my psyche. This realization sent me on a whole new trajectory.

EMOTIONAL INTELLIGENCE

The Dalai Lama once said, "All sentient beings possess awareness, but among them, human beings possess the greatest intelligence. Subject to a constant stream of positive and negative thoughts and emotions, what distinguishes us as humans is that we are capable of positive change."

I read this excerpt from the book *Emotional Intelligence 2.0*, which I picked up in an airport bookstore on my way back home to Buffalo shortly after Miss Fitz's memorial.

The term emotional intelligence was just starting to become mainstream and I hoped that the book would offer some wisdom. I was being hard on myself after Miss Fitz's memorial, for not having the language to communicate my feelings, so I decided to buy the book and give it a read.

Up until this point in my life, I was not sure what it even meant to be emotionally intelligent. The word "emotion" was never discussed in my house. If anything, any expression of emotion was deeply frowned upon. *Stop crying, or I'll give you something to cry about* was the usual response to any outburst, so I was beyond curious about what the book had to say.

Miss Fitz's passing was bringing up all sorts of new feelings, ones that I hardly understood. The book suggests that there are four different levels of emotional intelligence: emotional perception, the ability to reason using emotions, the ability to understand emotions, and the ability to manage emotions.

Before I could even start exploring what these levels even meant, I first needed to learn how to define the emotions I was feeling. This sent me on an even deeper dive. I got on the internet and typed "emotions" in the Google search bar. Images of a beautifully colored wheel appeared, as if they'd been designed to educate young children. Using all the colors of the rainbow to depict the spectrum of emotions, the wheel is divided into eight pie-like wedges, each having a core emotion in the center with a wide range of emotionally related feelings radiating out through the middle and outer layers.

This "Emotion Wheel," designed by an American psychologist named Robert Plutchik, became my golden ticket in helping me name all of the emotions—108 in all!—I'd never had the words to convey. The top wedge is yellow with JOY at the center. Moving clockwise, the next wedge is light green for TRUST, dark green for FEAR, then light blue for SURPRISE, dark blue for SADDNESS, purple for DISGUST, red for ANGER, and finally orange showing ANTICIPATION.

The Emotion Wheel became my road map while practicing the exercises in the *Emotional Intelligence 2.0* workbook. The knowledge I gained was liberating. Through daily journaling and listing my emotions, I began to heal some of my old childhood traumas. I began to notice some of the cycles in my behaviors and to recognize triggers hidden deep inside me. Introspection became a new daily practice, and I was beginning to better understand myself and those around me. I was beginning to forge a new path.

As I began learning about myself, I began holding myself more accountable. This did not lead to perfection, by any stretch of the imagination, but it gave me a reference to the work that I needed to do in order to heal. The one hundred and eight emotions became my lifeline, and I knew there was no going back.

CHAP

5

DAY FOUR: JUNE 13TH, 2021

Life is a moving target.
Like the North Star,
It is ever changing.
Today, Polaris,
Perfectly nuzzled in between
Ursa Major and Cassiopeia.
The next orbit around,
Another opportunity,
For a new North Star to shine.

CENTER OF THE UNIVERSE

On day four, just four miles before the rapids began, we eddied out where the Green River meets the Colorado. The sandy beach played center stage for our intimate wedding day. The Center of the Universe. A confluence. A sacred place, where two people and two rivers become one. We were welcomed by sandy shores. We drank in the love that was slated to be ever-lasting. We professed our most heartfelt desires and promises that day.

Grabbing his tattered notebook, Chason opened to the page where he had written his promises to me. He recited his vows first. In a loving and kind voice he began to read them aloud:

I vow to,
Love and Respect
Guide through turbulent highs and scrappy lows,
striving to find the goldilocks flows through life.
To honor and cherish.
To break trail to the top and ensure your well being on the journey.
To listen and to learn.
Embrace the growth mindset.
To trust and be trusted.
To communicate with compassion, direct and without fear or judgment.
To be open and receptive.

Next, I began to read my vows out loud. I prefaced that the 80's pop song *Promises, Promises* by Naked Eyes had played on the radio right before I sat down to write them, and that the theme may have stuck.

I promise to love you unconditionally and to be faithful, both physically and emotionally.
I promise to make you a priority and to love you without judgment.
I promise to support your journey and to continually work towards a reciprocal relationship.
I promise to be empathetic to your feelings and to be open and vulnerable in the process.
I promise to love you forever and to honor and respect you, for all of our living days together.

We agreed that these were reasonable and acceptable, then sealed the deal with a kiss.

Then Chason asked if I had written my acknowledgements. This was something he had made a point to mention weeks prior. I had been confused by what he meant, but I did not ask for further clarification, so I read what I'd come up with from my journal:

I acknowledge your desire to be at the top of your game, and that in order to achieve that, you must expose yourself to dangerous situations.

I understand that your self worth is deeply rooted in your ability to be proficient in the mountains.

I promise to support your choices and hope to always come to fair and reasonable compromises with you in regard to our adventures through life together.

I appreciate your willingness to slow down and guide me through the mountains while you navigate me through life's rough waters and I am grateful to have you by my side as we summit life's most remote peaks.

You are caring, compassionate, engaging, competent, smart, calculated, risky, adventurous, witty, emotional, grounded, sometimes moody, composed, well spoken, knowledgeable, comforting, sexy, loving, loyal, trustworthy, healthy and you are my family.

When I looked up from my writing, Chason looked awestruck and bright. He began to laugh as he read his outright.

Good evening my love,
I am so excited for our future together. You inspire me to love wholeheartedly, to be grateful for what we have, yet mindful of the possibilities. Your determination is palatable. We are blessed by our community of friends and family that your beautiful soul attracts.

"Wow," I said in fright, as we laughed at my long-winded insights compared to his beautifully written words. Then I closed our ceremony with a blessing and a prayer.

For the highest good in mind, and with the best of intentions for all of those concerned, thank you, Gaia, for blessing us with such love and such grace. We feel deeply supported by you, as we stand in awe while our dreams and aspirations manifest into a life more grand and prosperous than we could have ever imagined.

Afterwards we wrote our names into the sand using a whittled beaver's stick. A contract of sorts.

Just Married
JCL CPR
6/9/21

ALWAYS LANDING ON THE SAME COORDINATES

As we floated away from the Center of the Universe, vows and promises aired, Chason looked at me and asked, "Why did you marry me? And not Andy or Christofer?"

I answered with my own question. "Why did you marry me, and not Galena or Emily?"

That's when Chason said, "I still had so much to learn after I dated them both."

I nodded my head, understanding his sentiment. Then I replied, "Well, you've always made me feel safe. Whenever there was a big adventure on the horizon, I'd ask if you were on the roster. If you were in, I was in. It's strange. I've always felt looked after when I'm with you, and you've always just felt like family to me."

Chason looked at me with deep admiration and said, "That's the greatest compliment anyone has ever given me."

We floated away from the sandy shores relishing in the moment. I felt so much relief. I had a life partner. I was no longer alone in this big scary world. Chason Russell was my husband. He would be my protector from here on out. I felt like the luckiest woman in the world.

Chason, meanwhile, had sprawled out under the bimini, looking over Papa's river map, trying to gauge just how far we had gone. We hadn't been paying much attention, but there was a specific camp just after the confluence with an undisclosed trail that he wanted to explore.

I was at the back of the boat, steering our way down the lazy river, noticing how the still water perfectly reflected the riparian zone. Tamarisks lined the river banks, their feathery pink fronds waving in the soft breeze in juxtaposition to the red clay cliffs standing tall and proud behind them.

Lost in thought, I couldn't help but think about the confluence of life events that had cosmically evolved over the last couple decades and what a wonder it was that Chason and I always seemed to land on the same coordinates.

Me from Buffalo. Him from Telluride. Us meeting at the Observatory, years after I had heard about the place. Then both of us living and working together in Aspen.

It felt like we were bubbles swirling in the same eddy. Round and round we went. Always in the same steady current. Always on the same trajectory. Whether we knew it or not. Bound together by life's karmic ties. Destined to be.

So much life had happened for us both to end up where we were. So many relationships had to unfold for us to see the potentialities in one another.

All in divine timing, I reminded myself. *Remember, the universe laughs when we make plans.*

Soon we rolled up to the sign marking the beginning of the real rapids.

DANGER

CATARACT CANYON

HAZARDOUS RAPIDS 2 MILES AHEAD

We stopped for a photo, then cinched down our gear. We were about to be greeted by 15 miles of 26 Class III-IV rapids. The calm ripples that seemed endless just days before began to turn a tide. River-wide waves began to engulf our raft, lapping us up like a dog licks its owner. The river splished and she splashed, cooling us off from the incessant desert heat. Rolling solo, Chason chose the clean lines and left the spicy ones for another day. We were in it. We were soloing Cataract. No one else but us.

*****

IDAHO VIA CESSNA

It was 2008, the end of my second ski season in Telluride and time for our community to plan our off-season exploits. Instead of applying for river permits that year, a few of us decided to go rogue and head to Idaho to paddle several famous rivers—the Selway, the Middle Fork and the Main of the Salmon, and the Payette Rivers—before high season closed the rivers to anyone who hadn't drawn a lucky permit.

Our friend Captain Colorado, a pilot, was spearheading the trip. He was a regular at Las Montañas, and I had gotten to know him pretty well, serving him bourbon on the rocks and chatting about rivers. Captain was a stoic, strapping guy, always dressed in a white collared shirt and a brown leather bomber jacket. The name Captain Colorado fit him nicely.

Andy and I were invited, as well as YB, Tanya, Annie, Chason, and Chason's new girl-friend Emily, whom I hadn't gotten to meet yet. YB, Andy, Annie, and Chason were all qual-ified Class V kayakers, seasoned at exploring deep river canyons. Their paddling skills were next level, and I was excited to have their safety skills on board.

Emily, Tanya, and I were less experienced, for sure, but had enough river knowledge to hold our own. Captain was an experienced oarsman, and was psyched to have us girls on board for the first half of the trip, as we were going to help him power through some of the bigger rapids on the Selway. I was excited to step out of my comfort zone, and be humbled by the bigger whitewater in Idaho.

I was also excited to connect with Emily, because she and I had basically switched places. She'd moved from Telluride to Salida the same week I moved from Salida to Tel-luride, a year and a half earlier. The two of us were constantly being asked if we knew each other. When we finally met, we both laughed that we'd probably passed each other multi-ple times on the highway, moving across the state.

She and Chason had just recently met on a Grand Canyon trip. I had heard about her in-famous river piñatas, filled with kinky adult party favors and hilarious river schwag. I won-dered what tricks she had up her sleeve for this adventure.

The first river on the docket was the Selway, a classic 48-mile stretch that would take four days. The Selway was unlike any other place I had ever experienced, a remote slice of earth with no one else in sight. The fresh snow melt pierced your skin when the waves hit your face. The water was big and the granite was a stark white. Emerald green moss hung from the pines, and there was a fresh hatch of purple butterflies that gave the whole gorge a fern-gully-feel. The water was so clear you could drop your water bottle straight into the river and take a drink.

Next, we landed Captain's Cessna on a tiny landing strip at the Indian Creek Put-in to run the Middle Fork and Main of the Salmon. His four-seater plane was loaded with kayaks and the *S.S. Sexy Time*, Emily's little 12-foot raft that she, Tanya and I were slated to R3. *Sexy Time* was quite the name and we did our damndest to live up to it.

Emily took the paddle captain seat fresh off the bat. She had done the Middle Fork of the Salmon before and said there wasn't much to worry about the first day we put on the river. As she was in the back, steering S.S. along, Tanya and I noticed that she had gotten side-tracked, looking for god only knows what in her dry bag.

We looked at each other, then back at Emily as the water banked around a 90-degree turn, causing a river-wide surf wave to form across the river.

Tanya and I both yelled, "Emily! We are about to go sideways into that huge surf wave! Correct the boat!"

But before she could get her poop in a group, we were dropping into the wave sideways, perfectly positioned to flip.

GRRRRGLGGGGRRRRRGLGGGRRRRGLLL!

Nothing like a Class II swim at the very beginning of a week-long river trip to start things off on the right foot. None of us had been prepared to flip, and most of our gear was not tied down. Sunglasses were lost, day bags got wet, and the whole situation left us feeling real un-S.S.*Sexy*.

We drank from our river booties, a ritual that must be performed after any flip or swim, this one only two miles into our 100-plus-mile trip. With our first flip behind us, we deemed ourselves Team Struggle Bus for the remainder of our I-da-ho adventure.

It was early spring, in the Frank Church Wilderness, and the mountains were still holding a lot of snow. The water was cold and there seemed to be a constant headwind blowing upstream. One afternoon the winds got so rugged that S.S. was having difficulty making any headway. Gusts were blowing us upstream, and we found ourselves ascending the river. Chason saw our situation unfolding, and without saying a word, docked his kayak onto our tiny craft, then took charge in the back. As hail began to pummel down, he started singing camp songs and counting paddle strokes to lift our spirits. Like a true camp counselor, he led us down the river until the storm let up.

When we reached the bend where the Middle Fork flows into the Main Salmon, we girls traded in our paddle raft so we could kayak the more mellow stretch of whitewater on the Main Salmon. Annie was our fearless leader and we followed her down the river like baby goslings, bobbing up and down, as the Class III wave train led us to the take-out in Riggins.

Captain's Cessna, along with the other small plane we chartered to help shuttle our gear, opened up a whole new world of chasing rivers. Car shuttles, trailers, runway locations, opened and closed roads, river levels, river hazards, menu planning, and camp locations were just a few of the logistics that needed to be figured out on each leg of the exhibition. We loaded rafts, kayaks, and goodies into the planes, and ran as much whitewater as we possibly could. The challenges of coordinating such details really allowed for us to get to know one another, and allowed space for us to navigate the newly forming group dynamics that were setting us up for a lifetime of adventures together.

Our group included many strong personalities, and I was impressed with Chason's level-headedness and ability to subtly take the lead, especially when flood waters began to encroach on one of our campsites and we had to pack up late at night and relocate to higher ground. His ability to shepherd the group while making game-time decisions began to truly shape my deep trust in him.

After our trip to Idaho, Andy and I decided it was best to take a break. On paper our lives made sense. We both loved to ski and paddle, but in real life we saw things through a much different lens. It was a difficult break, as we were making a community together, and we did our best to keep things amicable. In the end it was for the best.

Not much time passed before I met someone else. We'd met briefly years earlier, while I was in school down in Durango. His name was Christofer, and he too had grown up in Telluride and was dear friends with Chason and my old roommate Buck from Boulder. Christofer spent his summers in Alaska commercial fishing. He was home for a few weeks on break and we re-met on the river. Our love quickly budded and I found myself in a new relationship.

MISTY MAIDEN

From 2007 to 2010, I moved from house to house in Ophir, a tiny mountain hamlet three miles off the Million-Dollar Highway south of Telluride. Ophir is accessed by traveling through multiple slide paths, and in the winter it is advised to give someone a heads-up that you are on your way home. During snow and wind storms it is also a good idea to have an avalanche transceiver turned on before you make the turn into the tiny town, but once you have made it home safely, you are just footsteps from the most epic backcountry skiing any ski bum could ever dream of. In the summer of 2010, after two years of dating, Christofer decided to buy us a home there, with his fishing earnings.

From 2007 to 2011, Chason and Annie ran the Telluride Academy's Kayak Program, but in the fall of 2011 Emily asked Chason if he'd like to leave Telluride for a caretaking position in Aspen. The job would include adventure guiding, and Chason was intrigued by the opportunity. The two of them had been dating long distance since the start of their relationship and they both needed to figure out where their relationship was headed.

From the outside, their new life together in Aspen seemed to be more taxing than rewarding. When their clients planned a bike trip through Europe in the summer of 2013, the two of them asked if I'd come and be their third wheel for a recon mission to iron out some trip details. I had been working as a road bike guide and could bring some experience to the table. I was a little hesitant at first, as I'd witnessed their relationship struggles over the years, but I didn't want to pass up a trip to Europe. Christofer would be fishing in Alaska, so I decided to accept their offer.

Chason and Emily were organizing an itinerary from Amsterdam to Brugge, Belgium. We decided to tack on a ski adventure while we were there. Our friend Howdy was doing a ski patrol exchange in Tignes, France, and he had a line on a cheap place for us to stay. He and his girlfriend, Galena, would make perfect ski guides for our adventure.

Galena and Chason, in fact, had been high school sweethearts, and shared a long history together. They remained good friends after their breakup, and I admired and appreciated the love and respect they both shared for one another. I had done some river trips and some ski adventures with them over the years and I was always impressed at how their friendship prevailed.

Unfortunately, Galena tore her ACL just hours before our plane landed in Geneva. It was a total bummer. I was really looking forward to skiing with her. With Galena out, morale was low, but that didn't stop Howdy from being an accommodating ski guide. He had arranged for us to ski the Tarentaise Tour, a classic off-piste ski adventure that takes you to three different ski resorts through the French and Italian Alps. It's not a feat for the faint at heart, 68 kilometers in total, across three 3,000-meter peaks through the Tignes, Champagny la Plagne and the Les Arcs ski areas. The tour offers huge descents that were mostly obtained by skinning, using cable cars, trams and taxi cabs. Howdy organized the whole day, and even reserved us a five-course meal in the middle of the excursion. After skiing off the first two summits, no one complained about the cassoulet, foie gras, espresso, and grappa that were being delivered to our table overlooking the pristine alpine landscape.

It was an epic way to see the Alps. For our final approach, we caught the last tram cart up to the top of the Aiguille Rouge. It was late in the afternoon, and the alpenglow was starting to show its glory. We had gotten beta that the rising temps that day had increased our chances of encountering some wet slides on the southeasterly aspect we planned to ski last. A *pister*, as the French call their ski patrollers, informed us that the south side of the Aiguille had already slid earlier that day, so it should be safe to go. We started our ascent up the final pitch, when a female pister came running out of the patrol shack in hysterics.

"Avalanche, Avalanche!" she yelled, waving her arms in wild concern.

Howdy and Chason continued marching up, unfazed by the manic bellows coming from down below. Howdy had gotten intel that the slope on the other side of the Aiguille had indeed slid, but that the bed surface was good to go. The two of them nimbly tiptoed their way up on the supportable crust of snow, cresting the top of the ridge, barely impacting the path. Emily's bootpack, however, broke the crust of the creme brûlée and left us wallowing in custard. Beneath the burnt sugar surface was nothing but rotten snow, which left us drowning in unsupportable granulated snow crystals.

I was behind Emily, and I began to get nervous as I watched her struggle. All the while I could still hear the French pister yelling down below "Avalanche, Avalanche!" while she wildly waved her arms at us to stop.

Emily managed to make it up, but I was tired and exhausted, and I was starting to bonk. The five-course meal had crushed my momentum and this last taste of dessert was taking me down. The woman's screams were not helping the situation. Like an egg, I began to crack, and by the time I reached the crux move, I was completely shelled. All I wanted to do was turn around and ski back to the bottom of the ski area. I had no interest in skiing the Aiguille Rouge from the top and I most certainly didn't want anything to do with the terrain, if had indeed slid.

Tears began to well up in my eyes, as Chason turned to look down below the ridge. As he peered down on me, he shot me a look. It was a familiar look. A look that he had given me many times before. Like the time I was struggling to paddle in the wind on the Main Salmon, or the time I was about to drop into the San Joaquin couloir, or the many other times I was completely freaked out, and he was completely comfortable, and I needed some coaxing to conquer the beast in front of me.

Basically, this was not a new scenario for the two of us. And there we were again, in the same predicament. It seemed like he was always there when I was completely scared out of my wits, doing something that was just slightly out of my comfort zone. Over and over, he had to come and calm me down and cheer me on so I could conquer my fears.

"I'm turning around," I said.

"If you ski down from there, you'll end up in Italy. We have a car waiting for us down here, in France!" He said assertively, as he aggressively pointed to the other side of the mountain with his ski pole.

"I don't care. That woman down there is screaming at us to *stop*. She's still down there! I am tired. I am scared. And I am done. I'm skiing down this side," I said stubbornly, starting to wipe the tears from my eyes as my goggles began to fog up.

"It's like Misty Maiden up here. Misty fucking Maiden!" he said, trying to convince me that it wasn't as scary as I was making it out to be.

Misty Maiden is a beginner blue run on the Telluride Ski Area. I didn't care. I didn't budge, and the sobs were beginning to build.

Then, changing from pointing his ski pole, to banging his ski pole on a nearby rock, he continued his coaxing.

"You are not turning around, it's like Misty fucking Maiden up here! Misty fucking Maiden!"

Then, before I could react, he dropped his ski poles, leaned over, and grabbed me by my jacket, hoisting me up and over the last approach of the climb.

"*RRRRRRUUUFFFFFFFFFFFF!*" was the only sound I could hear coming out of his mouth.

It was a pretty macho move for him, and I was surprised by his strength. Skinny-strong, I thought.

Once I collected myself and looked past the huge avalanche debris that ran just to the right of the terrain we were about to navigate, I realized he was right. It would be just like skiing Misty Maiden, minus the huge blocks of frozen ice chunder and avalanche debris we'd have to ski around.

The relief that came once I made it to the top of the Aiguille sent me into a state, and I decided it was time to tell a joke.

"Did you hear about the French bakery that burnt down last week?"

Confused, he just looked at me and said, "What are you talking about?"

I quickly replied, "Yeah, all that was left was the brie. Get it? Debris? The brie?"

He started to laugh and we were back to having fun.

Misty Maiden became the tagline for most of our jokes from that day on. Whenever I was scared or something looked too big to ski, or too scary to run, or too steep to climb, he'd say, "Misty fucking Maiden!" then somehow I'd muster up the courage and forge ahead. Trusting him, just like that.

THE ALEPH

After six days in France, Chason, Emily, and I traded in our skis for three rented Dutch-style Omafiet bikes and headed up north to Amsterdam. The Netherlands is a cyclist's paradise. The streets and sidewalks are designed for biking, never having to worry about curbs or cars. There's a flow. A palpable pulse of traffic. A cadence that never stops, and if you do, you can be sure to cause a traffic jam.

It took us a few days to figure out how to circumnavigate the concentric ring of roads that make the city. As you ride them, you feel as though you are peeling through the layers of an onion. Without fully stopping our bikes, we'd try and read the street names, which were more like trying to read a sentence. Each sign occupied as many letters as the English alphabet.

We also had a lot to do before venturing out into the tulip-filled countryside. Emily, a creature fueled by figuring out logistics, was fired up to impress their clients. Watching her plan was like watching a tornado spin its way through a Kansas cornfield. You certainly didn't want to get in her way, but boy could she get the job done.

We were staying at the Andaz, a bougie hotel with an Alice in Wonderland theme, owned by friends of Chason and Emily's clients. Enormously tall ceilings give the illusion that you've just fallen down the White Rabbit's hole, welcoming you when you walk in. With doors both large and small and garden tea parties around every corner, we felt like a cast of Alice's about to bike through her mysterious Wonderland. After many mad tea parties were had and numerous bicker sessions went unresolved, I couldn't help but question the viability of my wondermate's romantic relationship. As we biked our way through the Netherlands I found myself thinking about what the Cheshire Cat had said to Alice: "Never let anyone drive you crazy; it is nearby anyway, and the walk is good for you."

After we finished our tulip tour, we ended up back where we started: at the Andaz. As Emily spun around the Wonderland lobby, ironing out last-minute details, Chason and I found ourselves playing around in these tall tulip-shaped enclosed chairs. While we were twirling back and forth in our trippy flower pod arrangements, we made eye contact, rolling our eyes at the frantic planning happening all around us.

Suddenly it felt as if we were caught in Paulo Cuelho's *Aleph,* a book he and I had discussed many moons before on another kind of trip, in another kind of land. The Aleph, as Cuelho describes it, is a known point of energy, where you can feel all of the vibrations of the universe in one single moment. It's an experience where the present, the past, and the future are all happening at once. It's not something you can necessarily explain. It is more of a feeling, or a knowing, than anything. The moment was brief, and it was profound, and we both felt it. Maybe it was the tulip bud or maybe it was the intoxicating Amsterdam hash. Either way, the moment left us both feeling spun.

CONFLUENCE OF NUPTIALS

The three of us made it back to the States just in time for a wedding on the river. My dear friend Mama Bear was marrying her beau, Big Water Willy, another fearlessly skilled kayaker. A gathering of fifty friends were gearing up in Moab to run the Green and the Colorado Rivers. Twenty-five of us girls were slated to run the Green, while twenty-five guys ran the Colorado. We wouldn't meet again until the third day, at the Center of the Universe, where we'd float the remaining stretch of Cataract Canyon as one big happy family.

Emily, Chason and I got back two days before the I do's, and the three of us were in charge of the food shop. There we were, straight off the plane, running around the big box grocery in Grand Junction, food shopping for the masses. It was like a scene straight out of the reality show *Supermarket Sweep*.

Emily called out grocery items as Chason and I raced around the store, throwing two of everything into separate grocery carts, then labeling it all "1" or "2" as we shuffled the goods into bags and threw it all into the car, still packed with ski and bike gear from our European adventure.

We arrived in Moab just in time to meet all our favorite river runners and divvy up the menus. The ladies headed to the Green, the guys to the Colorado. Each team had six rafts loaded to the brim with food, booze, and kayaks. It was a bachelor/bachelorette party for the ages.

While floating the lazy Green River, we bachelorettes decided it best to each be given a number for safety. After leaving every beach, or after a few hours of debaucherous fun, someone would call out, "Number Check," and we'd count off "One, two, three.." until all 25 of us were accounted for.

In the midst of these count-offs we devised an impromptu choreographed singalong, involving a topless chorus of river antics. Upon one countoff rehearsal, we noticed a group of bikers riding along the canyon wall. An unusual site, so deep in the gorge, but they were riding the White Rim Trail, a famous 100-mile bike ride that follows certain sections of the Green River.

We thought it appropriate to give the bikers a sneak peak of our river dance. But mid-show, a turn in the river crept upon us. As the current began to pick up, we realized that our floatilla was about to slam directly into the canyon wall. Mama Bear got on the engine in hopes to miss the collision, but instead of putting the motor in reverse, she sent our rafts full throttle into the canyon wall.

BOOM!

All fifty of our itty bitty titties got tossed from our dance party positions, sending us tumbling into the wells of our rigs.

Again, Mama Bear attempted to get us back into the current, only to slam us once again into the wall. It was quite the sight, I am sure, for the bikers up above, and it sent us into hysterics.

Aside from the collision, we made it to the Center of the Universe in one piece. We arrived before the guys so we decided to set up the kitchen and do one last rehearsal before the bachelors arrived.

Hours later we greeted the guys topless and in unison. Our river dance was applaud'ed with shouts and whistles, and we noticed that the guys hadn't come empty-handed either. On Big Water Willy and the boys' journey down the Colorado, they'd foraged house-sized tumbleweeds and collected hoaps of driftwood to keep us warm for the next few nights.

Stan spiked the punch and set the tumbleweeds ablaze. You could see our fires from space as all of our LSD-inspired spirit animals came out to play. We were all lucky to make it out of the canyon alive. Chason later confessed that the guys only consumed the beef, bourbon, and bacon from the menus we'd packed so neatly into their boats.

By the end of our epic adventure, I had spent over thirty days with both Emily and Chason. I was grateful for the journey, but drained from their work dynamic. It was plain to see that the two of them were in the midst of a power struggle, and I wasn't sure they would be able to work it out.

THE ALLURE OF THE ROARING FORK

I returned back home to an empty house. So much had happened that spring while Christofer was away. I had just skied the Alps, rode bikes through the Netherlands, and celebrated with our closest friends on the most epic river trip ever. It seemed like so much life was happening without him that I questioned whether or not I wanted to continue living life as a third wheel while my own plus-one was away six months a year.

In the fall of 2013, I decided if Christofer wasn't going to give up fishing, I was going to have to make a change. I decided to leave Christofer and Ophir behind, and went in search of greener pastures. I moved thirty minutes west to a little farming community.

Gardening had shifted from being my modality for mental health to a way of making a living. In 2010, after moving to Ophir, I built a small greenhouse and began a community composting business. The business grew and I began a hub-to-spoke operation, collecting food waste from local restaurants and processing it at three different locations: on the west end in Norwood, atop Hastings Mesa, and the third continued at the Ophir Trash Barn. I also began collecting residential food waste weekly at the Telluride Farmers Market. Meanwhile, I also started a 6,000-square-foot biodynamic garden and began selling fresh produce at the market. Soon I was growing so much food with the amazing soil I was creating, that I decided to collaborate with other local growers and started a pop-up farm-to-table business, hosting fancy dinners all around the San Juans.

I was living my dream life of sustainable endeavors, but my business ideas were not so financially sustainable. After years of working around the clock, I was barely scraping by and in the winter of 2015, I decided to try out for the Telluride Ski Patrol. I needed to take the National Ski Patrol Outdoor Emergency Care certification class to be fully eligible for the position. While doing so I fell hard for the academia involved in the training, and after finding out how much I'd get paid as a ski patroller, I realized I'd make even less than farming. So, I decided to pivot.

Nursing was a profession that paid, it satisfied my new academic interest, and it offered a schedule that would allow me to maintain my outdoor lifestyle. I decided to enroll in classes at the Colorado Mountain College in the Roaring Fork Valley, hoping to be accepted into their nursing school program.

I had a few friends in the valley. Our friend Stan, whom I'd met in Durango when I first met Christofer all those years ago, had just married a woman named Cat, who was born and raised in Carbondale. Stan was splitting his time between Silverton, guiding at Silverton Mountain, and in the Roaring Fork guiding for Aspen Alpine Guides. Chason and Emily were still living in Aspen, but the two of them had split shortly after we returned from our Europe trip years ago. As it turned out, they were better co-workers than romantic partners.

Emily had married a physician's assistant she met after breaking her ankle, kayaking Slaughterhouse Rapid, shortly after her and Chason split. And Chason was keeping himself busy volunteering for the Aspen Mountain Search and Rescue team and also acting as head coach for the Aspen Valley Ski Club's Big Mountain Program.

The Roaring Fork Valley seemed like the perfect place to pursue a new career path. I figured it would be an easy transition from Telluride, since the valley had five ski areas to choose from and two hospitals that I could potentially work at once I graduated. I thought I'd conquered my fear of loneliness and that I would be so busy with schoolwork that the lack of friends would help me stay focused on my studies.

Boy, was I wrong. The solitude left me feeling suicidal once again, and dark thoughts began to creep in. *Why am I here? What am I doing? Why does everyone else have their lives figured out, while I am over here, all alone? I've failed at every relationship I've ever had. I failed at composting. I failed at my farm-to-table business. I am such an idiot. I am so miserable. I am so tired. I don't want to do this anymore. I will never have anything figured out. I am just going deeper and deeper into debt every day that I am here. Dad was right. School is such a racket. I don't want to do this anymore.*

I was 34 years old and caught in a complete victim narrative. I started alienating myself from the relationships I had back in Buffalo and in Telluride. Deep down I knew that if I didn't seek out professional help, I would wind-up hurting myself. So I decided it might be time to try out therapy.

In the process I fell down Alice's rabbit hole, finding a host of modalities to heal my pain and suffering. These modalities could be done all on my own, and I could find them for free online. Like Alice, who needed to fall in order to realize her true self, I began opening myself up to teachings on Buddhism, acupuncture, tapping, chanting, and breathwork. All of which granted me to a new arsenal of healing tools.

My newfound practices somehow moved the negative energies I was experiencing, and the discipline and practice brought on a new sense of empowerment. My suicidal thoughts began to shift as I became more curious. I started seeking classes in the area, and found a summer gardening job down the street from my new apartment.

A boutique yoga studio had just opened, and the owners purchased a one-acre plot of undeveloped land in downtown Carbondale with the intention of offering a community garden space. They needed some green thumbs to help build up the soil and start the planting process.

An old acquaintance from Telluride had moved to the Roaring Fork to manage the large endeavor. She had worked for a restaurant that composted with me. She knew my credentials and hired me on the spot. It all felt so serendipitous.

The two of us worked well together brewing compost tea, planting native flowers and transforming the stark desert-scape into a peaceful public garden space. It was healing to have my hands back in the dirt, and I began to feel like I was a part of something bigger than myself. I'd work all day while listening to nursing lectures, and while gardening didn't pay all that much, the dirt was working her magic. My spirits began to lift.

Sometimes Chason and I would go for a ski or a bike ride or a paddle after I got off work. Whenever we got together, we would discuss how hard it was to make new friends in our thirties, and that life in Aspen just didn't feel the same as it did in Telluride, where our sense of community was so strong. We began connecting on a deeper level, having conversations about our own journeys and in these conversations, we found ourselves on very similar spiritual paths.

I was surprised to learn that he, too, had found meditation and mindfulness as solid, healthy coping mechanisms to help heal his past. I felt an overwhelming connection when I realized that he, too, was doing the work to better himself, and I found comfort in knowing I wasn't alone on this new path of self-discovery. While having these intimate conversations, Chason began feeling more like family than just a dear old friend.

CHAPTER

6

DAY FIVE: JUNE 14TH, 2021

How can I be substantial if I do not cast a shadow?
I must have a dark side, if I can be whole.

— Carl Jung

THE RIVER GIVETH, AND IT TAKETH AWAY

As the river calmed, so did our nerves. We had survived the rapids, and the sense of accomplishment overwhelmed us both. As we began to float downstream, I could hear a roar coming from around the corner. We had just pulled off the shore and, although I'd tightened down the straps on all the drybags and Paco pads in my area, I noticed Chason's captain's boxes were both wide open, and nothing in his zone was strapped down. I also realized he wasn't wearing his PFD. Instead it was hanging off the back of the boat, dangerously close to the motor. Before I could ask him if he'd strapped in any of his gear, we were getting jostled through a series of big waves. We had a loose ship and we were not rigged to flip!

"Uh oh, I forgot there were a few more rapids," he said with a shit-eating grin. "We still have 27, 28 and 29. I forgot they come shortly after a brief bout of flatwater."

We made it through the turbulent waters without any carnage and with everything still accounted for. We both giggled at our cavalier re-entry when Chason confided a truth.

"You know, everyone thinks that I have it all figured out, but really I have no idea what I am doing. I really don't!"

I didn't believe him, but I let him have his moment. I trusted Chason with my life, like no one else in the world. Regardless of whether he knew what he was doing or not.

Just then, I noticed a bunch of swallows diving and swooping all around our boat. I looked up the canyon wall and saw the exposed carcass of the Paradox Formation housing the nests of hundreds of swallows.

I thought it was the perfect time to tell a joke: "If a stork brings a white baby and the raven brings a black baby, what brings *no* baby?"

Chason looked at me and winked. "The swallow," he answered.

We had been trying hard to make a baby. I'd never wanted children before Chason came into my life. The traumas of my own childhood were too raw, but seeing him with our friends' kids literally made my ovaries throb. He was so patient and so kind and so fun that I couldn't wait to see him be a dad.

We had gotten a positive read on a pregnancy test that April, just three months before our elopement. We were so thrilled at the idea of starting a family that Chason called his mom right away.

"Mom, Jess is pregnant!" I overheard him say in a proud boisterous voice. It was a tone I hadn't heard before. In most cases, Chason was a humble man, but the pride in his voice when he announced this news to his mother was affirming. We were going to have a baby.

His declaration made me anxious, but his excitement calmed my nerves. Chason didn't know the etiquette for sharing news like this. My experience was that one should wait until after the first trimester to tell anyone, as there is a high probability of miscarriage in the first three months. Against my better judgment, I decided to spill the beans and tell my mom as well.

That week I came home from work to find Chason standing at the stove, cooking us up some tamales. His favorite midweek dinner plan. When I opened the door, he turned to me and asked, "What do you think of Vestal?"

"The mountain?" I replied.

"No, if it's a girl. What do you think of the name Vestal?"

"Well, I never heard of anyone named Vestal before. Where did you come up with that?" I asked, secretly thrilled that this was what was on his mind.

"Well, it's the most beautiful mountain in the state, so I thought it would make a great name for a little girl." And just like that, we were thinking of baby names.

*****

A few weeks later, we decided to do a river trip down Westwater Canyon on the Colorado River. The first trimester being a finicky one, it was hard to say exactly how far along I was, but I couldn't have been more than seven or eight weeks pregnant. I remembered seeing a timeline that compared gestational age to the size of fruits. If my calculations served me correctly, my baby would have been about the size of a pomegranate seed when we launched the river.

I figured, *What harm would it be, to go down the river with a baby the size of a seed inside me?*

I was going to row *S.S.* while Chason kayaked his hard boat. We were on a trip with eleven rafts and five kayaks. I decided to hang back and run sweep, as I did not want to get caught up in the madness of all the other boats. The river was running 2,000 cfs, a super low level for Westwater. I hadn't seen the river that dry in almost fifteen years. I was feeling a little anxious about all the exposed rocks, particularly on the Class IV Skull Rapid. Skull has been a notorious nemesis for me. At certain levels I would grease my line, but at higher or lower levels, I often got engulfed in its fury. Before we left on this trip, I made sure I got some beta on the cleanest line to take at this low-water level.

As we floated the flatwater leading up to the rapids, we passed by a rookery of large nests high in a cottonwood tree. A mile or so down river, I saw a Great Blue Heron gracefully taking flight each time our rafts approached. Calm and deliberate, his massive wings flapped slowly and methodically to other wading grounds. The GBH, always a true presence of ease and grace. Two emotions I was trying to embody as we crept closer to the rapids. I watched as the heron found its next fishing spot and said a little prayer to the river gods for safe passage ahead.

As I approached the 90-degree bend that creates Skull Rapid, I saw carnage unfolding.

An 18-foot cataraft was riding the canyon wall vertically, its tubes completely emerged out of the water. I watched in wild wonder as both the captain—a competent oarsman—and his passenger fell from what seemed to be about two stories into the raging water below.

Then I noticed that the nine-foot MiniMe carrying a strong R2 team had flipped over, dumping its passengers into the mess of boulders that lay ahead. As my eyes scanned the wreckage, I noticed another raft getting violently surfed in a giant hole. Both of the captain's oars had broken in half, their splintered remains thrashing in the frothy white wash.

In the midst of all of this, I struggled to find my bearings. The line I usually took had disappeared. The river's low volume was exposing large sharp boulders, both to my left and to my right. As if reading my mind, I heard Chason yell, "*GO LEFT!*" pointing hard left with his paddle.

I froze. The left line did not look clean. It looked manky and jagged, but Chason's urgency snapped me out of my trance. I braced myself and dug both oars deep into the swift current, but it was too late. My right oar popped out of my hand. Before I could recover, my boat slammed into a rock dead sideways. I did my best to high-side, but the boat flipped in an instant.

I found myself trapped under my boat, which was being cheese grated along the rock that had flipped me. I struggled to find my way out from underneath, only to see that I was headed straight towards another SUV-sized rock. My fully loaded raft was not far behind me. *WHAP-BAM*! Again, I found myself sandwiched between my boat and a rock, being ground up and down and back and forth until eventually the current let us both go.

As I began to get smeared along the rough surface of the rock, I noticed Chason helplessly paddling right beside me. His eyes were the size of silver dollars, and he was in a complete state of panic. As soon as I got my bearings I climbed onto the stern of his kayak and he quickly paddled me to shore.

That's when I felt a gush of blood run down my legs. Not from an injury, but from deep within my insides. I knew at that moment that I was no longer pregnant. The intensity of the loss hit us both hard. We both mourned the loss openly, and learned our lesson in sharing the news too soon.

HELL'S ANGELS AND THE DEAD

After I told Chason my swallow joke, I noticed a faraway look in his eyes.

"What are you thinking about?" I asked.

"I wish you were still pregnant," he replied simply.

"So do I." I wanted to lighten the mood, so I added, "Well, all we can do is keep on truckin'," then gave him a wink.

To change the subject, I asked, "What was it like growing up in Telluride? Back in the early days?"

"Oh man," he said with a mischievous look. "It was the wild west back then."

Then he lit up.

"Back in '87, the Grateful Dead came to play in Town Park. I think I was about seven. Town turned into a complete scene. We were living up on Alder Street. You know where that big purple house is, on the corner? Papa built Garrett and me this cool tree fort. The Hell's Angels showed up and decided to camp right below it. Right under my fort. I was so pissed. All I could think was that I needed to get them out of there, so I went outside and found some rocks, then posted up in my bedroom window and shot them down with my slingshot. I've never been impressed with bikers or motorcycles ever since."

Damn motorcycles, was all I could think.

*****

I had a love-hate relationship with motorcycles. On a visit home to Buffalo the summer of 2016, my dad and I went out on a motorcycle ride. I was garbed in all of my mother's Harley Davidson gear, and we had met up with a few of my dad's friends along the way. We made a pit stop at a local greasy spoon for lunch. My dad took one look at the menu, told me to order him the Number 3, then went outside to smoke a doob.

When my dad was out of earshot, a big tall ZZ Top–looking character with multiple ponytail holders keeping his thick gray beard together leaned over the table and asked, "So, where'd Jimmy pick you up at, honey?", insinuating that I was my father's latest side piece.

"Uh, he didn't pick me up. I'm his 35-year-old daughter, and this is all of my mother's gear," lifting my arms and showing off my mom's latest Harley wear.

The rough and tough biker just nodded, then went back to his business.

Shaking my head in disbelief at the situation, I ordered my dad the Number 3 and got myself the Number 5, then headed outside to avoid any more awkward conversation.

Later that summer, back in the Roaring Fork, my mom called to tell me that my father had found me a white 2003 Harley Davidson Sportster, and that he was on his way to pick it up. My relationship with my father was a complicated one. He has a hard time expressing his love through words, and instead his love language is gifts. I had always loved riding on the back of his motorcycle with him, so he thought it would be even more fun if the two of us could ride together on our own bikes.

I went back to Buffalo that fall to pick up the bike. I loved learning how to ride with him, in the safety of the big beautiful cemetery behind my parents house. I enjoyed the rush, cruising at speeds of 20-30 miles per hour. I especially loved motoring past all my friends who'd left this earth too soon. I'd think of all the fond memories we shared as I passed their graves, remembering how much they meant to me and how much fun we used to have.

As much as I loved the motorcycle, I would get totally freaked out as soon as we hit the open road. Going 20 mph was one thing, but revving the motor at 65 mph in traffic was another. My father could see my trepidation on our final ride together, and the last thing he said as we loaded up the shiny white bike onto the trailer for me to tow out to Colorado was, "If you kill yourself on this bike, I'll kill myself." Not the most encouraging words, I thought to myself, as we tied her down.

DREAMS AND PREMONITIONS

By 2015 things seemed to be going better for my brother Kevin. Several years earlier, he'd met his fiancee, Bernadette, while working at the Monarch Ski Area just outside of Salida. She worked as a server at the mountain lodge and he worked back-of-house as a line cook. After a few years of dating, he asked her to marry him while they were visiting her family back in New Hampshire.

Bernadette's mother Facetimed the entire proposal while my mother, brother Michael, my sister Elizabeth, and I all sat quietly on the other end of the line. I'd never seen my brother happier than I saw him that night.

Bernadette had just finished her Sommelier 2 certification while Kevin was due for a large installment of his injury settlement. They both wanted to start their lives in a place where they could afford to buy a home with some land.

In the winter of 2017, they decided to leave Salida and move back to the east coast.

They found themselves living in wine country. Ithaca, New York, seemed like the perfect place to realize all of their wildest dreams. Kevin had big aspirations of opening an Airsoft field, hosting survival games. Bernadette was working in a fine dining restaurant where she had creative freedom over the wine program.

Kevin was never in a better place. He wanted to start his own family and felt it was important to face his past before starting a new future. He purchased a Harley Davidson, hoping to heal the wounds he had with our dad. His bike had all the bells and whistles. It was painted a matte black and had running lights that illuminated all the colors of the rainbow.

Early that spring, I received a package in the mail from Bernadette. It had a DVD of the movie *Bridesmaids* with a lovely note asking if I would like to be in her wedding party. I was so honored and called the two to congratulate them.

"Can you believe I'm getting married?" Kevin said, jubilant over the receiver.

"I can't," I said with great pride.

I was so proud of the man he was becoming, and I found myself getting emotional over the phone. It felt like he had turned a new leaf and that all his cards were finally falling into place. We ended the call with hopes for them to come out to the Roaring Fork for a visit. I was looking forward to getting to know my new sister-in-law better and so excited to celebrate the life they were building.

On May 31st, Memorial Day weekend 2017, an old friend from Telluride was working at a sushi restaurant in Aspen and invited me on a semi-commercial trip down the Slaughterhouse section on the Upper Roaring Fork River. The river was low, as the snow run-off hadn't really begun to flow.

The night before we put in, I had a dream. It was one of those dreams that sticks with you when you wake up in the morning. I was hugging a very large man. Bigger than my dad. The man was covered in tattoos, but they were blurry, like a watercolor. I couldn't make out any of the ink splotches, but I remember feeling deeply sad.

We were in a large space with many rooms. The other rooms were filled with people, and in every room, I noticed that everyone was somber and quiet. I remember hugging the man very tightly. When I woke, I could still feel the impression of the hug and the gloomy emotions I had been feeling in the dream.

Before I drove to the river put-in to meet my friend, I walked past the shiny white Sportster my father had gifted me. I hadn't ridden it much; the roads here were too busy, and I had no one to ride with. I remember thinking, *Why am I so afraid of my motorcycle, but not afraid of the river? They are both equally dangerous, aren't they?*

The previous night's dream was still heavy on my heart and I started to get butterflies as I got closer to the put-in. It was going to be my first trip down the river that season and I was going with a group of people I didn't know. The fact that we were going with a commercial outfitter didn't seem to settle my nerves.

I dressed in my drysuit and carefully listened to the safety talk. The outfit was run by a well-known debaucherous bunch of Aussies. I had given the speech many times myself and was amused to hear someone else give it. I listened intently to be sure that they'd covered all the bases.

We ran the river that day without any hiccups, but I still had a sinking feeling in my stomach before I went to bed. I did some breathwork and tapping to help calm my nerves, then fell asleep.

A little after midnight, the phone rang. It was my sister, Elizabeth.

"Kevin is dead!" she cried in horror.

My response startled the both of us: a deafening scream from the very depths of my body. All I could think was, *Was it him in my dream? Was I dreaming of his wake, before the accident even happened?* The coincidence frightened me.

Just like that, I had gotten the call. Life as I knew it would never be the same. My little brother Kevin was gone. He would no longer be around to drive me crazy or make me laugh or recite every line to every movie known to man. We would never line up again, oldest to youngest, for a family photo. His spot would never be replaced. He was only 32 years old. I was absolutely devastated. *How could you possibly love someone so much while being so absolutely irritated with them, all at the same time?* The sibling paradox.

Kevin had driven his new motorcycle off the road on the way home from a bar at 2 a.m. and crashed into a tree. There were no skid marks, and because of the text messages he had sent his fiancee Bernadette earlier that night, law enforcement suspected suicide. Though we will never know what exactly happened, I do not believe my brother intended to end his life that night. I believe he was upset and blowing off steam, and missed the turn on a fast new motorcycle on an unfamiliar road.

Bernadette was the first to find him. When he didn't arrive home, she used her Find a Phone function on her cell to locate him. She immediately started to perform CPR on him, but the trauma killed Kevin instantly.

Our family was not able to see his body after EMS brought him to the hospital. The only identifier we were able to see, days later, was the tattoo on the inside of his right index finger. It was a Gaelic expression, and I never knew the meaning behind the inscription.

If I could just have one more conversation with him, I'd ask, "What does that say?" and "What does that mean?" and "What does it mean to you to have it tattooed on your finger?" And "Why were you going so fast?" All questions I'd never get to ask.

Another incredibly unfortunate missed opportunity was that Kevin and my father never did get to go on that ride together. I believe the guilt of that missed opportunity still eats away at my father every day of his living life.

In honor of my brother, we had a motorcycle hearse carry him to his final resting place. A procession of RIP-roaring motorcycles followed, with my father riding my mother on the back of his purple flamed Harley Davidson Road King.

Shortly after laying Kevin's body down to rest, my father turned to me and said, "Sell that bike when you get back to Colorado, and use that money to buy yourself books for nursing school."

And that's just what I did.

THUNDER AND LIGHTNING

A couple months after Kevin's death, I was back in the Roaring Fork and he was heavy on my mind. I was bogged down with schoolwork, but was trying to stay on top of my wellness routine to ward off any dark thoughts.

I was receiving regular acupuncture treatments to move the stagnant energies that come with grief. After attending a very powerful appointment with my practitioner, she commented on the noticeable shifts of energy that took place in the room. When she placed and lit moxa, a resin made from mugwort, around my heart space, she mentioned that the movement of smoke it had created had caught her off guard. I too had felt this powerful shift.

After my treatment I was feeling extra "zingy" and sensitive to the world around me. I decided to skip the schoolwork and ride my cruiser bike to a hot yoga class. While riding to class, there was an electrical storm happening all around me. Bolts of lightning circled and I noticed dark storm clouds building at the summit of Mount Sopris.

A twin-summit mountain in the Elk Mountains that can be seen anywhere in the Roaring Fork Valley, Sopris is not the tallest mountain in Colorado. But it does have the most massive relief of 6,400 feet from the base of the Crystal River Valley to its summit at 12,965 feet. This relief creates a magnet effect for storm systems and can make for really dramatic lightning shows when conditions line up just right. The Ute called the mountain *Wemagooah Kazuhchich*, which translates to *ancient mountain heart sits there.* Legend has it that if the shadow of Sopris falls upon you, you will never leave the Roaring Fork Valley.

As I pedaled the few blocks from my apartment to my afternoon yoga class, lightning bolts were spearing down from the heavens. It felt as though Zeus was up there playing a game of Earth Darts, and I was hoping not to be the bull's-eye. While I was in class doing downward dog, I watched as lightning bolts appeared through the windows, giving the impression that they were piercing the bodies of all the other yogis in close proximity.

The combination of grief, acupuncture, and the energy of the storm were having visceral effects on my mind, body, and spirit. After class I raced home, having an unnerving feeling that there was potential for being struck as I made my way home on my rusty metal bike.

Home safe, I crawled into my leather chair and placed my computer on my lap. Then I opened up my text and leaned into the schoolwork I had been putting off. Before I knew it I was consumed with pathophysiology, and my mind began to settle.

WHAH-BAM! KA-BOOM!

In an instant, the heavens came roaring down and I heard the most startling, earth shattering, shake-you-to-your-core thunderclap right above my tiny little apartment. The vibration was so abrupt that it set off car alarms and rattled my dishes. It sounded like a bomb had just gone off inside my living room.

I leapt out of my cozy chair and volleyball-dived onto the ground, then army-crawled into my stairwell as my dog, Kayenta, scurried into my lap. We were both left terrified and trembling. I couldn't believe it. There I was, 36 years old and hysterically crying in my stairwell over a harmless thunderclap.

I reached for my cell phone and called my mother, who lives over 1,500 miles away. In a desperate moment of complete hysteria, I sobbed to her the entire story. This was an unusual move for me. Very rarely did I call my mother when I was frightened or needed help, but this was not a usual day.

My mother was perplexed on the other end, and in her special way, she found the humor in the situation. We both began to belly-laugh at my reaction. That's when she thought it was appropriate to share a story.

"A couple days ago," she said, "my highschool girlfriend Judy visited a medium, hoping to make a connection with her newly deceased mother. The medium said, "There is a young man here who would like you to tell his mother, 'Wait for the electrical event. That is when you will know I have passed onto the other side.' Judy knew immediately that this was a message from Kevin and called me as soon as the reading was over to tell me. I've spent the last few days walking around the house, waiting for the lights to flicker, or for the power to go out."

Mom and I both went completely silent, contemplating the possibility.

I broke the silence with a scoff, "You have got to be kidding me? Do you think that was him? Do you think that was his last practical joke on me? To send me groveling in the stairwell, sobbing like a child. Scaring the living shit out of me, with a thunderclap?"

But of course it was. Of course it was Kevin. Of course this was the electrical event he warned Judy about. The realization sent my mom and me into complete hysterics. Both laughing and crying at the same time.

"Wait for the electrical event. That's when you will know I have passed on to the other side."

He nailed it. Completely terrified me. Brought me into inconsolable tears. Then crescendoed it with a burst of belly laughter, shared between my mother and me.

I thought to myself, *Well, there you have it. That's the medicine. That's the gift. Be open to the signs. He's made his way to the other side.*

PURGATORY

I traveled home often that summer—both to be close to Kevin's grave and to reconnect with my family. I decided I wanted to share the electrical event story with Elizabeth, who seemed to be still grappling with Kevin's death. The two of them had a very special bond, and she was still deeply grieving. I was hopeful that in sharing my story I would bring her some closure. Unbeknownst to me, however, Elizabeth was still ravaged by recurring nightmares of Kevin, stuck in Purgatory, in complete and utter distress. The visions and emotions she felt in these dreams had haunted her since his passing.

Instead of gently approaching what I was about to share and listening to her experiences since Kevin's death, I carelessly doled out my revelations with the thunderclap and the "wait for the electrical event" experience that my mother and I had shared weeks prior.

"Kevin has passed on to the other side. Don't you see? The thunderclap was his way of telling me he has made it to the other side." I said, trying to convince my hurt little sister that Kevin was in a better place.

"How dare you say that," Elizabeth said. "He is not in heaven. He is in Purgatory. If he was in heaven and at peace, I would feel it. I don't feel him at all. That's why I believe he is stuck in between two worlds. Don't you see?"

My interpretation completely contradicted my sister's experience and quickly facilitated a very intense confrontation. In my mind Kevin had passed onto the other side. I believed he had experienced the "bardo" of Tibetan Buddhism, a religious concept I was loosely aware of where the dead undergo a cleansing of karmic debts before they reincarnate into their next life.

Elizabeth did not want to hear my story. It was not what she was experiencing or feeling, and my closure only made her grief more intense. She did not believe that Kevin was at peace. She did not believe that he was experiencing his next stage of passing. There was too much uncertainty surrounding the circumstances of his death that she truly believed he was still in Purgatory. To her, Purgatory was a place where souls go when they do not believe themselves worthy of eternal peace.

Elizabeth knew that this was much different than the traditional concept of Purgatory. She knew that Purgatory in the Catholic sense meant that the deceased experienced a period of suffering that is distinct from the eternal damnation of hell. She knew that in this suffering, the deceased are not punished, but rather purified of their sins, before their union with God.

But she believed that Kevin was still in a state of suffering, and that his suffering may be eternal and that he may never enter into heaven. She felt so strongly of this because she could not connect with him, as she could with others who had passed on. She was living with this fear, and this fear was real. And this fear haunted her.

In my effort to shine some light, I only shed more darkness. There was no beauty or peace to his ending. His story was tragic, and it was dark and it was terrible. A place where no light could, or should, be shed.

Instead of my brother's death bringing us closer, our contrast of beliefs were tearing us even further apart. My intentions to soothe my baby sister backfired, and I was devastated by her reaction.

This difference in our coping strategies in a time of grief intensified the wedge in my relationship with both my sister and my mother. We were not seeing eye to eye on how to honor and remember Kevin. I wanted to find lessons and gifts in his passing. But the idea of this only upset my family. They did not believe that there could be any lessons, and especially not any gifts in this time of deep mourning. The rift was growing and I was afraid I was drifting further apart from my family in the face of Kevin's death.

IT'S IN THE CARDS

I had my cards read shortly after my brother died. When I sat down in the fortune teller's booth, I made a point not to mention his death. I only asked if my parents were going to be okay. It was a vague question, but I wanted the mysterious woman to tell me what her cards had to say, without giving her too much information.

Before the fortune teller shuffled her cards, she asked me a very odd question.

"Why did you choose your parents?"

I thought it was the craziest thing anyone had ever asked me. I snarked back, "I didn't choose my parents. They just had me. How do you answer a question like that?"

The card reader stopped shuffling and explained, "Your soul chose your parents. You have karmic ties with one another. Karma is neither good nor bad. It just is. You choose your parents because there is still much work to be done. This is true even if your time together is very short, or if your parents decide they are not ready for parenthood, or if your mother passes away from the delivery. It is all destined to happen. Your soul chooses them. So why did your soul choose your parents?"

Just as quickly as she stopped shuffling, she started back up again.

I was not amused by the woman's question, nor was I amused with her explanation. It seemed off-topic and a bit too woo-woo for me to comprehend.

I watched carefully as she began shuffling her tarot cards and thought to myself, *Why in the world would I choose my parents? Why would I put my mom in that position? Why would I voluntarily choose all that generational trauma?*

Lost in thought, the card reader asked me to cut the deck. She neatly rearranged the cards, then began flipping them over one by one.

I was unfamiliar with the abstruse figures on the cards and their images frightened me a little. I felt darkness coming from the pictures and a chill began to rise on the back of my neck.

The card reader began interpreting her spread.

"You have lived many lives with your parents. The three of you are here, in this lifetime, because of events that have transpired many lifetimes ago."

Yeah, Yeah, Yeah, I thought. *You just said that.*

Then the fortune teller got real quiet and the expression on her face changed. With hesitation, she began to spin a story from the cards laid out in front of me.

"In another lifetime, long, long ago, your father was slain by a swordsman. You were not the one holding the sword, but you were the one who made the call for the hit. Your mother knew of your plan, and did nothing to stop it. That is why you are all here together, in this lifetime. To ameliorate the karma from this one event, which happened many lifetimes ago."

Goosebumps spread up my arms as I recalled a reoccurring dream I often had as a little girl. The dream took place at my paternal great-grandparents' house, right behind my grandparents' house. A mob of people were running through the streets with swords and torches in their hands. I would watch them from the safety of a window in the living room, as the mob rioted in the streets.

Then there would be a banging on the back door, like someone was trying to break in, and I would reluctantly go to the door and answer.

There, I would find a dinosaur-looking figure, injured and lying on the back steps. He was never scary, and always seemed to be in a lot of pain. He would explain that the rioters had stabbed him and he was in serious trouble.

Just as I would be coming down the back stairs to tend to the reptile's wounds, my dad would crawl out of the spiny, lizard-like body, as if he were wearing a costume. He'd explain that he was fine, and that I didn't need to be scared, and that it would all be okay.

I hadn't thought of that night terror since I was a little, but as the Tarot reader explained the cards, the dream crept up like I had just had it the night before.

Before my time was up, I asked the fortune teller if she could pose one more question to the cards. I asked her if I was going to be okay. I was still reeling from my brother's death, and I was worried about what my future would hold.

She shuffled her cards once more, then asked me to cut the deck. Then she stacked the cards back together again and began flipping them over one by one.

As I waited and watched, I saw the Death card cast its shadow. She placed it in the middle of the table, then she flipped over four more cards, placing them on each side of Death. I drew a heavy breath as she began telling me a new story.

She explained to me that there would be a man in my life who was going to die, and that there would be four people surrounding his death. She said that it would be abrupt, and that the four of us would all be deeply affected by his passing.

I immediately thought for sure the dead man would be my father, since he had fallen down a dark road of heavy drug use since my brother's passing. That would make the most sense, especially if there were four people deeply affected: my mother, my living brother Michael, Elizabeth, and myself.

The fortune teller insisted that it would not be my father, but another man who would be very near and dear to me. Then she explained that my father's death would not be sudden, like the man she saw in the cards, but slow and painful.

"He will not go easy," she said with certainty.

I left the table feeling emotionally exhausted. I felt like I had asked two very simple questions and been given many ambiguous answers.

Little did I know just how those cards would unfold.

CHAP

7

DAY SIX: JUNE 15TH, 2021

Hold fast to dreams
For if dreams die
Life is a broken-winged bird
That cannot fly.

Hold fast to dreams
For when dreams go
Life is a barren field
Frozen with snow.

— Langston Hughes

LOVE AT FIRST SIGHT

When Elizabeth was a very little girl and asked when her birthday was, she would say June *Fifteen,* instead of *June Fifteenth.* I've always loved that sweet memory of her. So on the morning of *June Fifteen,* I woke up with her on my mind. June had become a tough month for me. It was the month we lost Kevin, and the month that my two living siblings had birthdays.

Growing up, I had a special affinity for my baby sister. Six years younger, she had a certain innocence about her. When she was just six, she experienced a very traumatic dog bite that resulted in her having to receive multiple surgeries to correct her lower left eyelid, her upper left ear lobe, and her entire upper lip. The aftermath left her easily startled, and it pained me to see her endure so much pain at such a young age.

The morning of *June Fifteen* I was carrying a heavy heart and feeling far away from my family. I knew they were all so happy for Chason and me, but there was a piece of me that wished they could be there on the river with us celebrating our love. I also wished I could celebrate with Elizabeth on her birthday. As a remedy to my aching heart, I reassured myself that her husband, Dave, would have something special planned. He took such great care of her and it made my heart happy to know that she was with such a great guy.

Before I could mention my thoughts, Chason turned to me and whimpered, "How do you think our Sun and Little Moon are doing without us?"

*****

Sawyer was Chason's sunshine, and Kayenta was Chason's little moon. They were a handsome pair: Kayenta was a small German shepherd mix and Sawyer was an oversized Anatollian. I'd adopted Kayenta in the summer of 2010, after a neighbor lost her husband in a road-biking accident. One of her friends from out of town thought it would be a good idea to scoop up a feral mutt while getting fuel in the Navajo Nation and bring her to Ophir as a sympathy gift. But the widow was in no condition to take on the responsibilities of an untrained dog. Valerie caught wind of the foster situation and thought I should meet the mongrel.

The pup was just about six weeks old, with an ear full of ticks and a doggie STD that consumed half her tongue. The mangy mutt was in pretty rough shape, but I decided to take her for a quick walk up the Ophir Pass Road. I found her feisty and ferocious affect to be endearing, although she did frighten me a bit. She had a survivor's snarl and sharp pointy puppy teeth. While Valerie and I walked the mutt up the pass, the pup began to bite and snarl. Val decided to throw the mini beast onto her back and barked "No," in a low stern voice, showing the pup who was boss.

Dogs weren't exactly my thing after my sister's awful experience, but the feral pup's unkempt condition stole my heart. I felt a bit of me in her, with her unruly ways. As the rogue pup wiggled her way out of our grip, I could tell her temperament had potential to be tamed, and I decided to adopt her the following day. I'd remembered passing through a town called Kayenta on the Navajo Nation en route to the Grand Canyon, and thought it would be the perfect name.

Chason adopted Sawyer in the fall of 2012. Again, Valerie was involved. Her sister had done a brief stint in Colorado but decided to move back to Buffalo shortly after she arrived. She was downsizing some of the items she had acquired, including a pop-up trailer.

Chason thought this would be the perfect hunting camper. When he came to town to pick it up, Valerie's sister asked if he'd be interested in taking her dog, Sawyer, as well. Chason was a sucker for all four-legged creatures, and agreed to take the skittish dog off her hands. Chason showed up to Christofer and I's house in Ophir right after the transaction was made. Christopher and him were going to glass the mountains for elk, as it was just before the height of rifle season. I was curious as to how Chason had gotten suckered into the deal. Then I remembered who he was dealing with. Val's sister had a way about her, and could literally sell a glass of water to a drowning man.

As Chason hopped out of his big green Dodge, the overgrown Anatollian brushed past him, escaping this stranger's vehicle with no intentions of ever loading back up. Sawyer clobbered his way through mine and Chistofer's house, knocking over this and bumping into that with his oversized tail.

"How in the world did you go from picking up a trailer to adopting a dog?" I asked with complete astonishment.

"He looked like he could use a good home," is all Chason said, shrugging his shoulders with a matter-of-fact kind of tone.

The next thing I knew, Sawyer was lifting up his leg to mark his territory on a jacket that was hanging off one of my dining-room chairs. As I saw the steady golden stream pouring out of the untrained monster, I looked into my living room and noticed that he had done the same thing to each and every one of my house plants. Puddles of piss were spreading all around my house. I was horrified.

"Oh my God, Chason! Get him out of the house," I barked, while we shooed the untrained house guest out the front door.

Kayenta, who wasn't the friendliest dog in the neighborhood, was lying outside in the front yard, unfazed by it all. I thought it a little out of character, since she was still rough around the edges and wild as could be. Even after caring for her for two years, spoiled rotten with hikes and adventure skiing, she still acted feral and unruly. She'd growl and bark and show her teeth to any sweet canine that came close to our yard. I'd watch in horror sometimes while she'd be on her dog line, hair up on her haunches, posturing and ready to attack. The dogs in the neighborhood were only safe because after a few dogfights, Kayenta was now permanently grounded to the yard.

As Chason and I shooed Sawyer out the front door, I noticed Kayenta's gentle demeanor with him. Surprised and relieved, I turned back inside to start cleaning up the mess. A few minutes later Chason and I looked outside, wondering how the dogs were faring. We were shocked at what we saw.

Lo and behold, my aggressive attack dog and the skittish Anatolian were out front, licking each other's faces off. *Of course the two most unruly dogs on the planet would turn out to be the best of friends,* I thought to myself as I washed my hands of the mess Sawyer had made.

Chason stayed the weekend hiking game trails with Christofer, all the while having zero control over his new four legged best friend. Sawyer only obeyed, if Kayenta obeyed. When it was time for Chason to leave, Sawyer refused to load up into the cab of his truck. It wasn't until Kayenta loaded up that Sawyer quickly followed. I wasn't exactly sure how Chason was going to handle his new feral rescue without Kayenta leading the charge, but it wasn't for me to worry about.

As Chason rolled out of Ophir, Kayenta began to pout. It made my heart hurt to see her so sad. Every time after that, we would always laugh at how excited the two would both get when they saw each other, freaking out until the truck doors opened and they were re-united, free to run and chase and lick each other's faces off once again. Neither of us had ever seen our dogs behave that way with any other four-legged friends. It was *love at first bite.*

*****

MERRY CHRISMUKKAH

Our love story was not one of *love at first sight* or a story of *the perfect first night*. Our love story began with *love at first fight*. It was December 2018, and Emily was expecting her second child on the day of the winter solstice. She needed someone to fill her shoes while she and Chason's clients were in town, and asked if I could help him pull off the holiday season at their mountain mansion.

On Christmas Eve, I was preparing a meal to feed the masses while Chason took everyone out skiing for the day. Their clients' property sits on the west side of Aspen Ski Area. They regularly used snowmobiles to access the ski area via the Midnight Mine Road. Chason grabbed a few sleds, then made his way up the backside to the top of the gondola with the father and his two sons.

I was expecting Chason back around 4 p.m. to help with the final preparations for the 26 guests who were slated to arrive at 6:30. With no sign of him around 4:30, I started to get worried. I still had a lot to do and was running behind schedule. As I looked at the clock and the unfinished dishes strewn around the kitchen, my emotions began to flare.

I was feeling homesick, both for Telluride and for Buffalo. Cheffing it up in some fancy French kitchen wasn't exactly where I wanted to find myself Christmas Eve, but nursing school had run the bank dry and I needed the side hustle to keep me afloat.

Where in the world is Chason?

Stressed as the clock ticked closer to 6:30, I reached into the pantry and poured myself a glass of cooking wine. For all I knew, he was off on the back side of the mountain skiing fresh powder, having the time of his life while I worked away in the kitchen, pulling off a Chrismukkah dinner.

It was about 5:15 when he finally walked into the kitchen, reeking of blood and still in his ski gear.

"Where the hell have you been?" I asked, as I looked up from the unfinished charcuterie board.

"I found a dead elk on Midnight Mine Road, so I called the Department of Wildlife and they gave me permission to harvest it."

"What? You found a dead elk?"

"Yeah! I think a mountain lion just downed it. His guts were all eaten out of him, but his body was still warm, and there was still some good meat left on him."

"Are you friggin' kidding me?"

"No! After I got everyone down from the mountain, I went back up and rigged it to the back of my sled. I dragged it down to the garage then lifted it up with the skid steer and skinned it. His hind quarters are untouched, and the backstraps a still intact."

"You have got to be kidding me. And by the way, you are filthy!"

"I know, but guess what? There's enough meat for all of us to have elk in the freezer this winter," Chason said with a wink, knowing that this would be music to my ears.

"Ok. That's actually awesome," I said, kinda buzzed from the pantry wine and kind of excited about fresh elk meat.

"Alright, there is no time for you to clean up. I am super behind and I need your hands in the kitchen. Can you please help me finish cutting up these cheeses and meats for this charcuterie board while I finish prepping the lamb?"

Less than an hour later, guests began to arrive. Chason was still in his ski clothes, reeking of two-stroke and dead elk, *my favorite cologne,* and I was two sheets to the wind.

To our relief, we ended up pulling off the Holiday Chrismakkuh dinner, and as guests began to leave, I looked around and began to feel at peace. Maybe it was the pantry wine, or maybe it was how Chason always seemed to calm my nerves. Either way, I was starting to get into the Christmas spirit.

After we finished cleaning up Chason asked me if I wanted to go "rip some throttle" on his snowmobile to "blow off some steam." He wanted to return the remainder of the elk harvest back up to the kill spot, and I reluctantly said yes.

This wasn't the first time Chason had asked me if I wanted to hang out with him after we'd finished cooking and cleaning for his clients. I was starting to feel like maybe there were some sparks beginning to fly between the two of us. But we had a long history, and I was afraid dating would ruffle some feathers in our friend group, here in Aspen as well as back in Telluride. I had dated two of his good friends. And he had dated two of mine. But I agreed to go with him up the mountain to return the elk carcass. I filled up a Thermos with more cheap pantry wine, then threw on my ski clothes and met him outside.

Out on the sled, we rode the trails behind Aspen Mountain. As Chason ripped on the throttle, I squeezed his body close to mine. The mountain mansions were adorned with sparkling Christmas lights, and snowflakes glistened in the frigid air. We came up to an overlook and Chason slowed, killing the engine. He turned to me, as if to say something poignant, but instead he gently grabbed my cheek and kissed it. Startled at first, I looked at him in surprise, but in an instant I knew that his affections felt quite right.

We remained inseparable after that sleigh ride, and just two short weeks after our Chrismukkah cruise we anxiously told our family of friends the news. Upon hearing our story, I remember a few friends saying, "Well, it's about time", and "Of course, you two are dating. That makes total sense. You and Chason were always just one degree off."

We knew it would take some time for our friends and family to adjust, but their blessings meant the world to us. I remember thinking, *I guess it's true. Maybe we were always just one degree off? And as luck would have it, somehow we always manage to land on the same coordinates. How had we missed all the signs?*

WILL YOU BE MY VALENTINE?

Chason and I had been dating for two months when we went on a road trip to the San Juans to catch some storm skiing. First we headed to Silverton to ski with our good friends Stan and Kimmy. The storm was a doozy and we ended up kicking off some pretty big avalanches while skiing the expert terrain. I was grateful to have made it through the weekend without any casualties.

After skiing Silverton we headed to Telluride to see Chason's parents. The avalanche conditions had finally settled, and the backcountry was skiing really well. We were getting pounded with face shots, and the jubilation of the trip was intoxicating.

After a great day of skiing in Ophir, we went into town and grabbed a bite to eat. I was settling into the fact that we were going public, so to speak, but I still felt the eyes of judgment coming from some of our peripheral friends. It was true—our relationship was a tad incestuous. But Chason continually reminded me that it wasn't. Instead, he called it intimate.

We had created an unconventional life together, which is hard to explain to most. His comfort with it all eased my anxious mind, and when we got back to our friend's house that night he looked at me and said, "I think I am falling in love with you."

My insecurities got the better of me, and instead of returning the sentiments that I too felt so deeply in my heart for him, I said, "I want you to think of all the things you love, and share them with me when you've got it all figured out." It was a cop-out, but things felt like they were moving too fast. The love I felt for him was real, but I wasn't quite ready to take the leap of faith.

A couple mornings after we returned to the Roaring Fork, Chason left me a note on my kitchen counter. It was written on a beautiful piece of recycled paper and it said,

I Love.

I love the first rays of sun on a frigid morning

and finding shade in the intense heat of the desert.

I love cresting a ridge or rounding a corner

and taking in the scenery for the first time.

I love watching the darkness of a storm take over the sky

and the smell of rain nourishing the planet.

I love the sense of accomplishment

whether it is a successful descent or solving a problem.

I love when gear works flawlessly.

I love the rich colors of dusk and seeing the moon rising.

I love astonishing scenery, simplicity,

and the unmistakable smell of the river in the desert.

I love witnessing a fiery sunrise and the rich hues of dusk,

awe inspiring views and cactus in bloom.

I love the gentle warmth from a fire on a cold night,

deep conversations and celebrating accomplishments with good friends.

Most of all, I love having someone to share all that I love with.

Mountains and Canyons of Love to You,

Will you be my valentine?

Love, Chason

I went to his house later that night and returned the sentiments. I was finally allowing myself to let the love in. It felt wonderful and scary, all at the same time. Just another one of life's paradoxes.

I remember thinking: *Is this how it feels to be truly vulnerable?*

MY BOYFRIEND'S FERAL

Chason owned a trailer in Woody Creek, Colorado. The neighborhood is just a ten minute drive outside the hustle and bustle of Aspen. Running along the Roaring Fork River, there is a lot of charm, as well as a lot of history in the little town. Horses trot the perimeter of the neighborhood and there is even a hitching post in Chason's driveway.

The neighborhood was once home to the famous writer Hunter S. Thompson, who notoriously ran for Pitkin County Sheriff on the "Freak Power" ticket. Hunter S. was more publicly known for his gonzo journalism, where he believed that *absolute truth was a very rare and dangerous commodity in the context of professional journalism.*

The Woody Creek zone was also coined *Drug Alley Lane* to many old timers in the Aspen area, but today the streets have been gentrified and now there are more modular homes than there are mobile homes in the trailer park these days.

Had I not known Chason for twelve years, I would have hit the ground running the moment I saw the condition of his trailer. It was in complete and utter disarray. There were tall kitchen racks all over, littered with stacks of mountaineering gear. There were dirty dishes and unopened mail and garbage strewn all over the counter spaces. Mountains of dog hair were layered along the baseboards of every room, and his little trailer was in such a state that my heart broke for him instantly.

He had been telling me he needed to get organized, but I had no idea the mess he was living in. When I asked him how long his house had looked like that, he just looked at me with a blank stare and replied, "It just started to get so bad, I didn't know where to start."

My first night there, I cleaned a little spot on the counter so we could make dinner. When we went to bed, he turned to me and said, "I'm in awe."

"In awe of what?" I asked, confused.

"In awe of your ability to clear the clutter."

I told him I wouldn't come over again until he bought a vacuum cleaner.

A few days later, he called to let me know he had purchased a vacuum. He said he did a lot of research and it was the best one on the market. I thought to myself, *Okay this is a start.*

A true Virgo, my love language is showing affection through service. We had been dating about five months when Chason left town to take his clients on a road bike trip through Santa Fe and Taos. Kayenta and I were going to be taking care of Sawyer, and I decided it would be the perfect time to start cleaning up.

I picked up the clutter and organized everything into piles. Papers over here, gear over there, garbage where it belonged, in the trash. Then I went to town with the new vacuum cleaner. It was a beast and his unkempt house started looking like a cared-for home.

Once I could see the floor and the counters, I started the real cleaning. Wiping down the surfaces and scrubbing out the stains. Then I began rearranging. It was almost as if he had moved in but never found a spot to put anything. Once the Feng Shui was feeling right, I started opening drawers. More junk. More garbage.

Then I moved outside. I counted 19 kayaks in his backyard. Once I organized the kayaks to one side of the yard, I started picking up garbage. By the time I made a clear pathway, I had filled the back of my truck up three times. Each load went straight to the dump. I would pull in, get weighed, then happily toss all the garbage my new boyfriend had collected over his entire lifetime straight into the trash pile.

It was a purge.

It wasn't in Chason's wheelhouse to organize or throw anything away. He had collected and kept anything and everything he had ever acquired. Ski boots, ski bindings, bike parts, kayak padding, magazines, newspapers, lawn ornaments. You name it: if he collected it, he still had it. And if it looked like trash, that's where it went.

The clutter made me anxious, but the purge brought me satisfaction. Had this been any other human, I would have taken his hoarding as a deal breaker. But I loved him, and I wanted him to live in a peaceful and nurturing space. It made him happy to live in a clean house. He just didn't know how to manage it himself.

When Chason returned from his trip, he handed me two gifts. They were both wrapped neatly from the shops where he'd purchased them. He looked so proud of himself as he handed them to me. Before I even began ripping off the tape, he looked at me and said, "I think you're really going to love them." He was so sure of himself that his confidence threw me off guard and made me a little nervous. All of a sudden I began to feel a lot of pressure.

The first present was a hand-carved Japanese Hori Hori gardening knife. It was absolutely stunning. As I began to unwrap the second gift I could see the anticipation growing in his face. It was a simple porcelain teapot. Chason had perfected the art of making me a cup of tea in the morning. Not too hot and not too strong. *Goldilocks tea,* he liked to call it. The gifts were perfect, and I was floored. All I could think was, *Wow, he really knows me.*

After I took him on a tour of his new and improved house, he turned to me and asked, "Wanna move in?"

I moved in the following week.

TEN, NINE, EIGHT...

Chason and I began dating while I was still in nursing school. In May of 2019, shortly after I had moved in, I graduated and passed my boards. I had wanted to move back to the San Juans, and apply for a job at the Montrose Memorial Hospital, which was the closest medical facility to Telluride. But after much debate, Chason convinced me to stick it out in the Roaring Fork. He had a flexible job that allowed him to live a life he loved. He explained how important Mountain Rescue Aspen was to him and that he absolutely loved the watershed that we lived in. Against my bigger wishes, I applied for a residency position at Valley View Hospital in Glenwood Springs, as a surgical nurse. My application was accepted and I quickly began working long hours in order to learn my new profession.

After a busy day at the hospital, I arrived home to a delicious dinner Chason had cooked up for me. He'd often joke that I only loved him because he fed me. It wasn't that I didn't know how to cook. I just didn't have the time or the energy after work. So there was some truth to his jest.

After dinner, I showered and then got into bed. Chason had been acting peculiar for a couple weeks and I wasn't sure what was weighing on his mind. This evening was particularly unusual because he didn't climb into bed with me that night. *We always go to bed together,* I thought. *What is up with him lately?*

He said he still had some work to do. So I went to bed alone, worrying that he was worried about something. I had fooled him into believing that I was sound asleep, when he crawled into bed and began searching for my hand. At first I thought he was trying to put my arm around him, as he loved being *little spoon.* Instead I found him fumbling with my fingers.

"What are you doing?" I asked with sleepy eyes.

He had a piece of dental floss and a Sharpie marker in his hands. He was trying to slip the dental floss around my left ring finger, and was using the Sharpie to measure and mark it. *Is this his subtle way of sizing me up?* I thought.

A few weeks later, after hurting his back while moving snowmobiles for his clients, Chason decided to spontaneously book us a quick getaway to a family friend's vacation rental in Cabo Pulmo, Mexico. We'd been planning to go to Telluride to celebrate with friends and family at the Observatory, but Chason was in no shape to ski, so the spontaneous change of plans seemed like a good idea. I was working a lot of long hours at the hospital and didn't have time to participate in any of the planning. He bought the plane tickets, rented the car, and booked everything.

We flew out of Aspen on Chason's birthday, March 10th, 2021. I wanted his day to be special. A big storm was slated to hit the San Juans, and I could tell he was a little aggravated that we wouldn't be skiing for his birthday.

We made our way to our bungalow just in time to enjoy a sunset dinner on a veranda overlooking the Sea of Cortez. We had the catch of the day, then retired early and cozied in. It was the perfect first night to our five-day-getaway.

We awoke the next morning to gale force winds unlike anything either one of us had ever experienced. We laughed as we *weathermanned* the storm, taking videos of each other falling into the wind. The *playa* was an exfoliating experience, so we retreated back to the bungalow and found a deck of cards. We played rummy until we couldn't stand the wind any longer, then drugged ourselves into a sleepy slumber.

The next morning, a thick residue of hatch covered our entire bedspread. The roof was caving in on us, so we decided to go inland for a different kind of adventure. We found some hot springs in the little town of Santiago. Chason wasn't much for beaches, hot springs, or swimming, but he was a trooper. We found the hot springs and climbed up and around the rocks of the tributary until we couldn't explore any further.

We found a pool that was perfect for two, then spent the afternoon soaking in the sun. The scene was a mix of a lush rainforest and prickly desert cactus. The juxtaposition seemed fitting to Chason's unusual temperament. He seemed restless, anxious, and distracted—very different from his usual cool, calm and collected self.

At this point in our relationship, we'd been traveling together for over a decade. I could tell that something was off, but I couldn't seem to pry it out of him. I chalked it up to us not being able to ski the powder hammering everyone back in Telluride, mixed with the fact that we'd traveled all that way only to be shut down by the wind.

A day after our hot springs adventure, Chason awoke with a terrible rash. We assumed it was from the sun, so we went to every Mexican pharmacy we could find and tried every aloe and lidocaine cream we could buy, but nothing soothed his irritation. He was itchy and miserable, just another affliction adding to his already anxious affect.

The storm continued to rage on, and with no end in sight I decided to look at the local radar to see if there was a beach with no wind in the forecast. Cabo San Lucas, the touristy tip of the Baja peninsula, showed little to no wind, so I convinced him to leave cozy Cabo Pulmo for some much-needed beach time down south in touron-land.

Chason was visibly upset that we were bailing on the booked beach house. In his mind, we were walking away from a rental we had already paid for. But in my mind, we were headed to a place where the winds wouldn't blow us off the beach. It was my vacation too, and I was dying to get in the water and sit in the sand.

We drove to Cabo San Lucas, where high-rise hotels dominate the coastline and the infinity pools are plentiful. Chason, a world traveler to the earth's most remote places, was not impressed with the scene. When we arrived at our all-inclusive hotel, morale was at an all-time low. After getting checked into our room, I felt compelled to get to the beach and catch the sunset.

"Are you gonna at least put on a sundress?" Chason asked as I headed out the door.

Confused by his strange question, I answered back with an annoyed, "No!? Now hurry up! We are going to miss the sunset." Clad in my dirty old gardening sunshirt, tequila soda in hand, I left the room.

It was a classic Hotel California kind of evening. Hues of pink and purple illuminated the sky as the first glimmers of stars began to twinkle high above. The waves were crashing, making the sandy beach tremble at our feet. As a family on horseback paraded by, I tried my best to be present.

Chason, on the other hand, was fumbling with his phone, trying to prop it up on mounds of sand. I was already annoyed with his need to capture the moment when he interrupted my peace to ask if he could borrow my sandals and cocktail glass to help hold up his phone. Irritated, I reluctantly handed them both over.

"Ten, nine, eight...," he counted down, as he ran towards me, trying to snap a pic. While he clobbered his way over, the phone fell flat into the sand. I was not impressed nor the least bit interested in remembering the moment. I returned to listening to the waves crash and watching the colors of the sky change from a peachy orange to deep crimson purple.

Again, Chason propped up his phone, then began stumbling back to me through the deep sand.

He started counting down once again: "Ten, nine, eight..." I took my attention away from the waves and looked towards him with discontent. That's when I saw him drop down to one knee and say something to the effect of "you are my rock" and "I don't want to do this life without you."

His hands were trembling, and there was a quick shortness to his breath. I was so overwhelmed by his nervousness that I crawled over to him on my hands and knees in an attempt to comfort him.

In his ramblings, I don't believe he ever actually popped the question. I just hugged him while he went on and on about never wanting to keep a secret from me.

As we knelt in the sand holding one another, I pulled away and asked him," Did you just propose?"

"Yes," he said. "I mean, Will you marry me?"

"Is this why you have been acting so peculiar?"

He looked relieved. "Keeping this secret from you has been the hardest thing I've ever had to do," he explained. "I don't ever want to have to keep anything from you ever again."

Then he held out a simple band with a simple stone, and asked, "Jessica, will you be my wife?"

I slid the ring onto my finger and told him, "I would be honored."

I saw the Russell twinkle in Chason's eyes that night. He was beaming. He wanted a big wedding and wanted to throw a huge party. He wanted to invite all of our friends and family. I had never seen him so happy. I remember wishing he had asked me the first night we arrived, on his birthday, so we could have spent our days in Baja celebrating instead of him fretting over the perfect time to pop the question.

He said he had wanted to do it on the beach the first day we got there, but he was too afraid to take the ring out, for fear that it would blow away into the Sea of Cortez. Then he confided that he had his whole speech written down and he had been rehearsing it over and over again in his head the entire time we'd been down there. When we got back to our luxury hotel room he shared his words with me, written in his crinkled kayaking log.

Jessica,
Thank you for bringing calm and cozy into our home.
Cleanliness and ambition.
Honestness and Continuing Education.
You are a sparkle on a snowy moonlit night.
My landmark rock at the entrance of a turbulent and complex rapid.
Most of all you are my friend, my teammate, my partner and my lover.
I want to share the rest of this precious life with you.
Will you marry me?

After showing me the words he'd rehearsed but couldn't spit out, he explained that he had sent my mother an email asking for my hand in marriage the day before we left, but he hadn't heard back from her until a day ago. It was the middle of tax season, and my mom and sister own a tax preparing business together. They are both pretty difficult to reach all winter, until after tax day, which isn't until April 15th.

I laughed at the circumstances. Our trip to Baja had been the most stressful vacation we'd ever gone on together. All that time, I was worried that he was going to break up with me, when in reality he was stressing about not hearing back from my mother, and how and when to propose. I had it all wrong, and I couldn't have been more relieved or more excited for the life we were about to build together.

CHAPT

8

DAY SEVEN: JUNE 16TH, 2021

Dharma, like water,
is the act of opening to what is.
A letting go of the story.
A surrender to the present.
It is warm, so I am rain.
It is cold, so I am snow.
It is hot, so I am steam.
Dharma, like water,
is ever changing.
Always in flux.
A moving target.
An element of its environment.
It is a letting go of the story.
An expression of what is.
I want to be more like water.
In the flow, crystallizing, rising.
Open to the present, cleansing in nature,
the elixir of life.
Snow be it. I am water.
Let the light shine through me.
Showing all my radiant colors,
My true unique expression.
Free flowing and free.

LUPUS IN FABULA

On our last morning on the river, Chason awoke in a terror. I was surprised because we were in such a state of joy. He told me he was having another one of his vivid dreams. He was in battle, struggling to stay alive.

He seemed so rattled that I asked him if he was okay. That's when he decided it was a good time to share the story of his *wolf* with me. As he began, Chason grew somber, and his affect left me feeling a little uneasy.

"One evening," he said, "when I was about eight or nine years old, a silverish gray wolf came to visit me while I was tucking myself into bed. He stood austerely at the end of my bed, just staring. His eyes were black as stone and their power put me into a trance. We shared an exchange. The feeling has never left me."

Confused, I asked him to elaborate. "Were you scared when you saw the wolf? Did you feel like he was going to harm you?"

"It was more like a deep knowing," he continued. "Like this wolf was there to guide me in some way. But I wasn't sure if the path was going to be one filled with strife and sorrow, or one filled with joy and fulfillment. It was a mystery. But the wolf was there to let me know that he was with me. Whatever that looked like."

Then Chason asked the wolf, "Is this a dream?" But the wolf did not answer. And then Chason realized, "No. I am not dreaming. I am wide awake."

He paused his story, then started again. "My heart started pounding in my chest. And my hands began to shake under my covers, as soon as I realized the vision was real."

After Chason shared his wolf story, he lay quiet in contemplation. There wasn't really much to say, as I could tell he was working through something in his head.

That's when he said he wanted to share another story, about an unusual dream state he'd had back in May 2020. When he and two other friends escaped the COVID restrictions of the real world for a kayak adventure in the ancient lands of the San Rafael Swell, in Utah.

I remembered him being very excited for the trip, as he had never been able to catch the rare release of whitewater. Chason was still in an intimate morning state of grogginess and contemplation when he began. "The remote Black Boxes were gushing with frothy white-water that day. After miles of paddling the complex rapids, Mike Bone and I unrolled our sleeping pads to dream under the stars. The land beneath us had been hardly visited. The fissures and gorges that make their way through this section of earth are only experienced by the very few who can kayak the complicated rapids to get down into them. While we slept, I had a dream. I was there, on the same rock where I lay, but I was transported into a different time. There was war and bloodshed all around me. It felt so real. There were in-digenous people, all wearing loincloths and adorned in furs. Men were battling with bow and arrows. Spearheads, their ammunition. There was smoke and this thick musk of battle all around. It felt so real that I could smell it."

Chason closed his eyes as if experiencing the dream all over again, awakening all his senses.

"When I awoke," he said, "the dream weighed heavy on my mind. I turned to Bone, who was lying a few yards away. I wasn't sure, but then I decided to recount the experience with him. I did it in great detail."

"What did Bone say?" I asked.

"Bone said, with the same trepidation I was feeling, that he was there too! I couldn't be-lieve it. Yet I knew it to be true. The encounter left us both feeling uneasy."

Chason asked Mike, "Do you think we just traveled back in time, to a battle that had happened here before?"

Mike wasn't sure, but he was pretty positive, just as Chason was, a battle had transpired that night.

The energy of the dream was palpable. And it was no coincidence. The spirit of the land was sending a warning. A battle was upon them both.

The Italians have a saying, *lupus in fabula*, or the wolf in the fairy tale. Chason was Irish-Italian. He was also a Pisces. A true water sign. Chason was always in a constant battle with the dynamics of fantasy and reality, like two fish swimming in opposite directions. And just as there is always *a wolf in the fairy tale,* there is always an unexpected obstacle waiting just around the corner. Especially when you are a Class V kayaker, and most especially when things seem too good to be true.

INAUSPICIOUS CONFESSIONS

The last big crux of our expedition honeymoon was the Dirty Devil takeout. It is a river take-out with the potential to end any solid relationship, thanks to its mucky features and quicksand qualities. It was 103 degrees under the desert's blistering sun when we arrived at the dreadfully steep boat ramp. With oven mitts protecting our hands from the hot metal, we de-rigged our vessel of burning love, drenching our bodies in the river with each lap. We schlepped all our belongings back into the truck, and although we were covered in river muck, we deemed our mission a success. We celebrated with a selfie, then drove off into the sunset, saying goodbye to the desert, grateful for our safe passage.

As Cataract Canyon receded into our rear-view mirror, we faced re-entry as husband and wife. Chason and I often found ourselves in deep conversations when we had hours of windshield time. Driving home with nothing else to do but go deeper, we began discussing life and religion and our spiritual beliefs. Our lifestyle choices had brought us so much joy, but our unconventional choices had also brought us devastating loss and sorrow. Life in the mountains has a way of bringing deeper truths to the surface, and it felt only appropriate to discuss what our lives would look like moving forward. I wanted Chason to start considering me in his decision making. Especially because we were actively trying to start a family.

On our final leg home we drove over McClure Pass, along the beautiful Crystal River. The Crystal, named for its clear waters, is a Class IV-V river that runs from the top of McClure Pass to the confluence of the Roaring Fork. As winter thawed, the Crystal quickly became a springtime mistress in our relationship.

Chason had been paddling Meat Grinder, his favorite backyard rapid, since his early twenties. The upper rapids on the Crystal are only runnable a few weeks a year, during the spring run-off and Chason and his best friend Stan would run it as many times as their busy schedules would allow. Meat Grinder was one of the many river-related reasons Chason loved living in the Roaring Fork Valley so much.

The river was juicing at a stout 800 cfs that day. As we drove past the ominous Meat Grinder rapid, Chason turned to me and said, "I just don't feel like a Class V kayaker anymore."

I quickly replied, "Thank God, because it's super stressful being in love with a Class V kayaker."

We both chuckled, and with his confession aired, I felt a sense of relief. Meat Grinder was off the list of things to worry about.

*****

FORESHADOWING

Weeks prior to our elopement, Chason had been diagnosed with autoimmune hepatitis. He had been battling right-sided liver pain, weight loss, and fatigue for a year and a half, and neither a strict gluten-free diet, cutting out the booze, or supplements recommended by a highly respected natropath had helped. His liver enzymes were elevated and remained clinically high for over 18 months before the gastroenterologist prescribed a heavy-hitting corticosteroid. Chason was to take the medication three times a day for the next three years.

It was a trying time for both of us, having just lost a child in the early weeks of pregnancy, and then receiving his ambiguous health results. Upon his diagnosis, Chason picked up his year's supply of the steroid and continued on his way to the Rogue River, in Oregon, for a short work trip. In classic Chason fashion, he detoured en route to paddle some nearby Class V.

First on the docket was the famous Klamath River, a must-paddle California river whose four dams are slated to be demolished, returning the river back to its natural state. Chason was thirsty to experience the Klamath's thrashing rapids before the river flowed freely again, and what better time to do it than en route to a work gig.

After their successful trip down the Rogue with his clients, he and his fellow safety-kayaker buddy Casey headed to the Trinity River, a tributary of the Klamath and another must-paddle Class V run. Known for its massive gradient—dropping some 200 feet in a short two-mile section, with countless waterfalls, river holes and boulders—it is a section of river that only the best of the best can paddle.

But, as Casey would later tell me, Chason had not been on his game in California. Both the Klamath and the Trinity have numerous underwater sieves and river-wide strainers that could quickly kill you if you weren't on your line. After each gnarly feature, Casey would look back upriver to check in on Chason, only to find him flipped upside down, attempting to roll his kayak, or with his head dripping wet from having just gotten thrashed in a hole. Casey found it odd, because Chason had always been a river mentor to him, and had always been on his game.

Chason was no stranger to class V whitewater, but he was a stranger to the side effects of a heavy-hitting medication. When he returned home from that 10-day work trip to the Pacific Northwest, I hugged him, noticing that his body was already undergoing the changes that occur when you start taking a high-dose corticosteroid. He was filling out and starting to build back some of the bulk he'd lost since the start of his early-onset cirrhosis.

CHAPTER

9

DAY EIGHT: JUNE 17TH, 2021

Remember Dear One,
The hurting heart is a holy heart.
A cathartic moment is not a healing moment,
but an invitation to the healing process.
Healing is like an initiation.
If one allows the intimate and emotional feelings to emerge,
only then can one cross the threshold of healing.
True healing has a deep visceral feeling.
To engage in the work is not for the faint of heart.
It takes strength, character, courage, grit,
vulnerability and stamina to stand in the flames
of feeling everything that comes up.
Grief, if truly felt, can be one of the
most transformational experiences,
but one must be courageous enough
to open one's heart to its wrath.
The heart will only become whole again,
if one allows themselves to lean into the discomfort,
and feel all of the pain.

MORANING SMOOCHES

We got home from our honeymoon late in the evening and left the unpacking for the next day. I had to wake up early for a 12-hour shift at the hospital, and Chason had a busy day getting ready for his clients to arrive.

I woke up before the sun, dressed, made some tea, smooched Chason on the cheek, then headed out the door. As I climbed into my car, I realized I'd left my tea on the counter, so I went back inside, and decided to give my newly wedded husband one more kiss before leaving.

I grabbed him by his bristly unshaven cheeks and laid a soft gentle kiss first on his forehead, then on the tip of his nose and then one last lingering kiss on his big full lips.

"Mmm," is all he replied, his eyes still shut, tired from the week's adventures.

"Love you, husband," I whispered as I pushed out the bedroom door, my hot tea in hand.

"Love you, wife," he replied with sleep in his voice.

I drove to work in a daze. Re-entry was always hard after a river trip, but re-entry after having said our I do's at the Center of the Universe was even harder. I was scheduled to scrub in with an ortho surgeon for seven procedures that day.

As I walked into work, my co-workers congratulated me and asked to see pictures from our elopement. At the end of the day, the surgeon fist-bumped me and congratulated me on my new marital status.

It was a successful first day back. As I changed out of my scrubs, I grabbed my phone to send Chason a message.

An "I live you husband" misprint prompted an "I live you too wife" reply.

An "I'm running the Crystal River, be back to make dinner" text received.

Then crickets to my "Let's do something easy?" reply.

I figured Chason was running the lower section on the Crystal, called the Narrows, since he had just confessed that he wasn't feeling much like a Class V kayaker anymore. So I wasn't at all worried when I didn't hear back from him, as I figured he and Stan had made it onto the river and that his phone was safely tucked away in the cockpit of his kayak. There was no cell service on the river, so I figured I'd hear back as soon as they were back in town.

THE CALL

I got home a little before dark and grabbed the dogs for a quick walk. I was surprised not to see Chason cooking when I walked in, but figured he and Stan were catching up on the week's adventures. I grabbed Sawyer and Kayenta and we headed out.

The two of them were so in love, their bond was still so strong, and I was so elated with how all of our lives had turned out. It all seemed so perfect.

As I walked the soft surface path up on Post Office Mesa just outside our Woody Creek home, I got to thinking of all the things I was grateful for. I had married Chason. He was going to be my husband, and I was going to be his wife. I felt so lucky to be married to such a wise, reliable, competent, and calculated mountain man. He had always made me feel so safe when we explored the mountains together, and now he made me feel safe and secure in our new married lives together. A sweet feeling of relief rushed over me.

We had both come from troubled childhoods and difficult pasts. I remembered him saying early on in our relationship after a quick visit to his dad's house, "Well, neither of us came from a home full of unicorns, rainbows, and lollipops."

It was true, neither of us had had easy childhoods. It was something that had made our bond even stronger. The idea of being in partnership with a man who I'd known for so long and had lived so much life with, first as a friend, then as a lover, seemed like such a gift. Chason was no stranger. He was my friend turned best friend and now husband. I'd never felt so safe, or so secure, or so relieved in my whole life.

The dogs and I got back home, and I started to wash some dishes. I was thinking about what I could start making for dinner when my phone rang. I figured it was Chason, telling me he was on his way home, but the call had come from Stan.

Maybe his phone is dead, I thought.

"Hey honey!" I said.

"It's Stan."

"What's up, Stan?"

"I have horrible news," is all he replied.

"Don't even say it, Stan! Don't even fucking say it!" is all I could spit out.

"We ran Meat Grinder, and Chason is still in the river."

"What do you mean he is still in the river?!"

RUN GONE WRONG

Chason and Stan planned to meet up for a quick evening lap down the Crystal. Chason had the swagger one has post-honeymoon. While running shuttle, Stan later told me, Chason had bragged to him about how much babymaking the two of us had done while making our way down Cataract.

"Yeah, buddy," Stan had said in his thick southern drawl, nodding his head up and down in approval.

After running shuttle, a third paddler joined them—Alex, a mutual friend of both Chason and Stan's who had recently moved to the area. In their usual river dynamic, Stan and Chason decided to sandwich their new comrade in between them, Stan in the lead and Chason running sweep. The three snapped on their skirts and paddled out into the calm waters above the complex Meat Grinder rapid.

They ran the first section of swiftwater bobbing up and down, warming up their paddle strokes and finding their groove. After entering the dagger filled mess of rocks, Stan eddied out, lining himself up for the next crux move. Chason and Alex eddied out just above. Stan remembers wishing they had pulled into the same eddy, because that would have lined them all up perfectly for the next, must-make move.

Instead of motioning Chason and Alex into his eddy, Stan gave Chason the universal head tap, asking if they were "all good." Chason signaled back with a head tap, then the three of them peeled out of their respective eddies into the next feature.

Stan, in the lead, was running the next section of drops when he heard Alex yelling from behind, "Swimmer!"

Stan immediately paddled to Chason, right before the two of them got swept over a series of drops. Chason climbed onto the back of Stan's kayak, but just as the two of them were about to go over another jagged ledge, they were barreled into a large hole. The force of the hydraulic caused Stan's kayak to flip, and Chason got ripped away from the stern of the boat.

Stan nailed his combat roll just in time to see Chason getting flushed over the next big drop, his body immediately submerged by the raging flows. Moments later, Stan and Andy saw Chason's hand begin to rise out of the frothing water, his helmet just shy of the surface.

Stan eddied out behind Chason's body in an attempt to make contact, but in the process lost his paddle and had to make his way back to shore by hand. Once on land, Stan and Andy tried getting to Chason by using a throw rope, but too much time had passed, and Chason remained engulfed in the rapid. It wasn't long before Chason became unresponsive.

After two hours of failed attempts to recover Chason's body from the river, day had turned into night. Around 9 p.m., Stan and Alex drove back into town to deliver me the news.

CHAPTE

10

LIMINAL SPACE: JUNE 18TH, 2021

Meat Grinder
Game changer
Grief is not linear
Acceptance was my first response.
He summited Maslow's Hierarchy.
A peak of perfection.
The only mountain that matters.
He self-actualized.
Chason Patrick Russell
Cause of Death
Drowning
CPR
Irony

A MAN OF MOUNTAIN RESCUE

My youngest brother, Michael, was born on June 18, 1990. Nine years older, I carried him around like he was my own child. Now, on June 18, 2021, I wished I was back in Buffalo celebrating his birthday, hanging out with him and my niece Aadyn and my nephew Gabriel, playing Catan and hiking Chestnut Ridge to the Eternal Flame Falls. Anything other than what I was about to do.

Instead, at daybreak, I arrived at the river where Stan had last seen Chason. Like a flood, word had spread and our river community began trickling in, one raindrop at a time. By midday, over fifty people had arrived on the shores of the Crystal, offering assistance and advice to the Aspen Search and Rescue teams, who were doing their best to recover any clues of Chason's whereabouts.

I stood on the banks of the river as my long-time-ago boyfriend Andy and other kayakers snapped on their kayak skirts in a valiant effort to find any clues of him. The humming buzz of drones purred above the savage river below. As I observed the happenings all around me, I couldn't help but imagine Chason swimming in the manky collection of jagged, house-sized boulders.

The rapids exist because the river passes over a steep redstone wash full of gigantic loose conglomerate sandstone. The gorge continually flushes itself out every time precipitation runs through its soft steep surfaces. It's a rapid filled with underwater sieves, its shores riddled with strainers that have collected wreckage and debris. Chason was trapped underwater, like a twig caught in the current.

Although Stan stood steadfast in his account of their run, video footage showed no sign of Chason's body in the flows. As dawn turned to dusk, the official first responders—police, fire and Mountain Rescue—deemed it too risky to continue. The chiefs, sergeants, and leaders of each squadron approached me at the end of the day with defeat in their eyes. They gave me two choices; wait for the flows to go down and hope to find Chason when the river receded, in days or even weeks; or leave it to our own community of river experts to continue the recovery of Chason's body.

Chason had served on Mountain Search and Rescue Aspen for eleven years. The men who showed up that day were his comrades. I knew that if Chason were alive, he would be the one leading the mission. That realization gave the situation even more gravity. With full support, I chose option two. Our river community would conduct their own recovery, just as Chason would have done for any of those who showed up that day.

We were informed that if anyone else got themselves into trouble, our team of friends and family would be their only hope of rescue. I told them that I understood what they were telling us and that we would be as safe and cautious as we could possibly be.

Heavy in grief and disbelief, I perched on a rock overlooking the river. Like the heron we'd seen just days before while floating down the Colorado, my eyes fixated on the hole where Stan had last seen Chason. I couldn't help but think, "What were his last thoughts? Had he thought of me? Is his soul trapped in this place? Is he stuck in Purgatory?"

The rapid continued to rage on below, offering me no solace or hope.

NO MUD, NO LOTUS

According to psychology researcher Brené Brown in her best-selling book *Atlas of the Heart*, the ingredients needed to evoke the emotional state of shame include but are not limited to: secrecy, silence, and judgment. I grew up in a household where the daily rhetoric was "what happens in this house, stays in this house." That baked for a real sour-tasting recipe of shame, one that is deeply ingrained into my being.

When Kevin died, I was introduced to the work of Swiss-American psychiatrist Elisabeth Kübler-Ross. In her book *On Death and Dying*, she discusses her famous five stages of grief: denial, anger, bargaining, depression, and acceptance.

At that time, I had appreciated being introduced to EKR, with her neatly organized stages. Although they were not linear, they seemed like a tangible lifeline while riding the waves of grief. I felt like I could use these stages as buoys as I bobbed up and down in the watery seas of despair.

Guilt, shame and judgment were not discussed in EKR's book, and I thought this was strange because I was riddled with these emotions when Kevin died.

Why was he on his motorcycle, driving drunk, at 2 in the morning? I am so mad at him for doing this to our family. Then I would think, *I should have loved him more. I should have been there for him more. I should have advocated for him more.* But that was not our relationship. And that guilt and shame and self-judgment broke me open.

Was I the only person who felt like this after someone important to them died? Is this healthy? How do I work through these feelings?

I realized I still had a lot of work to do when it came to dealing with these emotions, and as I reeled in the depths of grief a toxic victim narrative came creeping back in. *Why me? Why not somebody else? What did I do to deserve all this loss?*

The Zen Buddhist master Thich Nhat Hanh said that most people are afraid of suffering. But he also reminded us, "Suffering is a kind of mud, to help the lotus flower of happiness grow. There can be no lotus flower without the mud."

It would be an understatement to say I was suffering when I left the river that day. With no sign of Chason, I began clinging to Elizabeth Kubler Ross's stages again. Anger, Disbelief, Bargaining.

Hadn't I already done this work? Hadn't I already traveled down this road? Hadn't I already learned enough of these life lessons?

In my re-hashing of old traumas, I felt like an unarmed target, in a nasty game of dodge-ball. Mud pies coming at me from every direction.

Mud pie to the face. Mud pie to the chest. Mud pie to the stomach.

I began experiencing fears of judgment from all spectrums of my world. From my family. From my friends. From my co-workers. From my neighbors. Waves of shame blew in, and an overwhelming shit-storm of emotions ensued as I drove home from the river.

First, I began judging myself for marrying Chason. Chason may not have been a drug addict, like my father, but he was addicted to skiing big lines and paddling Class V whitewater, which pretty much made him an adrenaline junkie, right?! And look how that turned out. He died kayaking Class V just eight days into our marriage.

Secondly, I feared Chason was being judged for the choices he'd made. I feared my friends and family back home were judging our lifestyle, just as I was doing as I reeled in the aftermath.

I was wet. I was cold. I was tired. And I was muddy.

I began having suicidal thoughts, more than I'd like to admit. I didn't want to live anymore. I didn't want to go on without Chason. The world was cruel, and I no longer wanted to live in it. I was judging my choices. Judging Chason's choices. Feeling guilty for blaming him for my suicidal ideation. Scared of what everyone around me was thinking. Feeling like I deserved to be a widow for marrying a man who put himself in dangerous situations regularly. I was in a complete shit-storm of mud pies.

But like Thich Nhat Hanh says, *It takes a lot of mud, and a lot of darkness, for the lotus to sprout and bloom.* And because guilt and shame and judgment became emotions, amongst all the others, that I was now facing in the depths of grief, I began clinging to one of EKR's later findings, *finding meaning.*

THE RECOVERY: JUNE 19TH, 2021

Make a nesting now, a place to which the birds can come,
think of your prayerful palm holding the blackbird's egg and be the one,
looking out from this place who warms interior forms into light.
Feel the way the cliff at your back gives shelter to your outward view
and then bring in from those horizons all discordant elements that seek a home.
Be taught now, among the trees and rocks, how the discarded is woven into shelter,
learn the way things hidden and unspoken slowly proclaim their voice in the world.
Find that far inward symmetry to all outward appearances, apprentice yourself to yourself,
begin to welcome back all you sent away, be a new annunciation,
make yourself a door through which to be hospitable, even to the stranger in you.
See, with every turning day, how each season makes a child of you again,
wants you to become a seeker after rainfall and birdsong,
watch now, how it weathers you to a testing in the tried and true,
admonishes you with each falling leaf, to be courageous,
to be something that has come through,
to be the last thing you want to see before you leave the world.
Above all, be alone with it all, a hiving off, a corner of silence amidst the noise,
refuse to talk, even to yourself, and stay in this place
until the current of the story is strong enough to float you out.
Ghost then, to where others in this place have come before,
under the hazel, by the ruined chapel, below the cave where shamans slept,
become the source that makes the river flow, and then the sea beyond.
Live in this place as you were meant to and then,
surprised by your abilities, become the ancestor of it all, the quiet,
robust and blessed Saint that your future happiness will always remember.

— David Whyte

LESSONS AND GIFTS

On the morning of June 19th, 2021, I woke up lying next to Valerie. I was blurry-eyed and confused. The previous day's events felt like an unthinkable and unimaginable nightmare. The truth of my situation became clear when I realized quickly when I knew I should that this world was made up of this miserable news of Chason gone, forever, or whatever that means. Instead of Chason, Valerie was beside me in our bed. I was living on the other side of my worst nightmare. I had lost Chason to the river, and I was having a hard time conceptualizing the depths of what this new day would entail.

Is this really my story? Is this really real? Is he really gone? Did Chason really die? Is he still in the river? Or have the currents dislodged his body from whatever vise had held him down? Has the river released him? Is he floating downstream for some fisherperson to discover, drifting among the rainbows and the browns?

Quickly and without warning, reality hit, and it hit hard. All of sudden I felt everything. The magnitude of what had transpired was visceral. My body began to tremble uncontrollably and my head began to ache.

He is not here. Valerie is here. He is gone. But where? We just got married. My dry bags aren't even unpacked yet. Our boating gear is still in the yard. My home is filled with family and friends. How did they all get here? Where did they all stay?

There was a somber commotion happening in my kitchen. I could hear dogs and the electric tea pot rumbling. I looked around my bedroom. We still hadn't unpacked from our honeymoon, and our boating gear was strewn across our floor, caked in sand and lofting the musty scents of river and consummation.

Funny how we held so much ceremony for a future filled with unknowns, when really we were unknowingly consummating a life apart. I consented to the start of a life, joined in matrimony. Not in separation. His parting was not consensual. I did not consent to losing my newly wedded husband. Yet, there I was, against my will, consenting to the search and recovery of his body. Whatever that looked like.

Being groomed for trauma from a very young age, my survival instincts kicked in. I grabbed Valerie by her arms.

"You have to help me find the lessons and the gifts today. You have to tell me one lesson and one gift when we get back here tonight. Whatever happens. I need one lesson and one gift."

Valerie just looked at me with her big brown eyes, tears welling up in the corners of her long curly eyelashes. Through her eyes I could see my own pain. She silently agreed and handed me a T-shirt from her overnight bag and put it on over my head. Without saying a word, she was doing what she had always done, taking care of me in my darkest hours.

One lesson. One gift. It was an urgent plea. A coping mechanism I had learned in the early stages of grieving Kevin. A way to honor those who have passed. A distraction of sorts, but also a healthy way to make sense of the nonsensical. I needed answers. Was it bargaining? Was it denial? Was it a ploy to find meaning? I do not know, but there needed to be a lesson and a gift that day if I was going to make it to see another.

Before we left the house, Valerie handed me a piece of paper. On it was a poem written by Rosemerry Wahtola Trommer, a Telluride poet who posts one poem a day on her website *A Hundred Falling Veils*:

This morning I woke
thinking of all the people I love
and all the people they love
and how big the net of lovers.
It felt so clear,
all those invisible ties
interwoven like silken threads
strong enough to make a mesh
that for thousands of years
has been woven and rewoven
to catch us all.
Sometimes we go on

as if we forget
about the net. Believing only
in the fall. But the net
is just as real. Every day,
with every small kindness,
with every generous act,
we strengthen it.
Notice, even now, how
as the whole world
seems to be falling, the net
is there for us as we
walk the day's tightrope.
Notice how every tie matters.

I fell into a complete free fall as soon as I received news of Chason's death, but the net had shown up. The copious amount of river expertise that showed up in those 48 hours was overwhelming. Not to mention the loved ones who hopped on planes and crossed state borders to reach me. Without the net, I would have drowned just as Chason had, into the deep, dark depths of despair.

THE PIXIE DUST FAIRY

Back at the river, our river family of experienced kayakers were converging, inventorying their gear and planning how to recover Chason's body. While everyone had collected every piece of rescue gear they owned, I found myself standing at the river's edge without even a PFD to keep me safe. I felt completely unprepared for what was about to unfold.

As our tribe dispersed to their assigned sides of the river, I found myself surrounded by the most important and influential women in my life. I had spent lifetimes with these ladies and there wasn't a face in the crowd that I didn't recognize. Then, as we were about to embark downstream, a strange and unfamiliar woman appeared.

I was immediately drawn to her. She walked straight up to me and embraced me in a way that felt comforting yet peculiar. She informed me that a mutual friend had sent her to come see me. She too was suffering, although from a very different, and very terrible loss. But in her knowing, I found solidarity. She had lost her son to suicide, and although I did not know her story, we knew each other's pain. So I opened myself to her.

After noticing the tremble in my hands, she informed me that she had worked closely with alternative medicine advocate Deepak Chopra and that she wanted to take me to the river to do some breathwork while the recovery teams set up their rescue devices.

We walked the grassy path upstream to the more tranquil currents of the Crystal, just above the rapids holding Chason's body captive below. The peacefulness of the water drowned out the chaos, and we began to breathe. I quickly fell into the comforting breathwork rhythms I knew so well, and felt my body begin to relax.

Once my nervous system calmed and the shaking ceased, the mysterious woman began explaining the contracts we make with our soulmates, long before we come down to "Earth School." She explained to me that Chason's contract had ended. That there was no comma or ellipses to his story. Only a period, to give any explanation for his departure from this life.

She encouraged me to let him go with peace in my heart and with an understanding that although he is gone from this physical plane, that he will always be here with me, because he is in me. She said it was a part of the death and dying process. And that clinging to him could hinder his path in the bardo, that Buddhist liminal state between death and rebirth. I wasn't exactly sure what she was talking about, but I already felt the need to let Chason go. To release him from the grip of the river. Figuratively, of course. I knew that his spirit needed to be free from this world so he could go on to the next.

She explained that Chason and I are tied together, as spirits. His passing, his leaving, was always the plan. We had made this agreement, not here in the physical world, but in the astral plane. He has finished his life sentence here on Earth. It was his intended time to go. She explained that he was at peace where he was now, and that I was still here, which meant I still had work to do.

I felt what she was saying to be true. *He self-actualized*, was my first reaction. *He transcended. He has reached his summit.* I remembered thinking that while we were on our honeymoon. The lack of distraction made his ascendance so clear. He's made it to the top. I remember feeling a little envious, as we floated down the Colorado, at how far he had come and thinking I still had so much work to do.

My mother sat with me, as the pixie dust fairy carried on and on with her woo-woo beliefs. My mother, who was raised Irish Catholic, took this woman's unconventional jargon with a grain of salt, but later she told me she started to hear a side to grief she was unfamiliar with, but one she had heard before, from me, while we were processing Kevin's death. It was a narrative that had driven a wedge between us in recent years, but one she was becoming more familiar with, as she sat with the family of Coloradan friends I had made over the last twenty years.

The pixie dust fairy left me with a few tokens that she believed would help me with the rest of my day. A sprinkle of organic tobacco and a dash of green herb, which she recommended smoking before I walked back down to the recovery site. She also anointed me with frankincense and rosehip oil, saying their essence would help calm my shaking nerves. I left the beach with a sense of gratitude and calm, then headed towards the recovery mission with my mother.

Before making it to the mess of ropes strewn across the river, I ran into Salli, Papa and Garrett. The three of them were sitting in camp chairs along the calm currents of the Crystal. The lazy beach is a perfect juxtaposition to the maze of house-sized rocks and strainers that make up the Meat Grinder Rapid that begins just steps away. If I didn't know them, it would appear that they were just there enjoying the serene and breathtaking views of the Crystal River Valley. Instead, as I approached them, I knew that they too were in the same depths of hell and grief that were plaguing me. I gave them all a squeeze, then told them I needed to be closer to the recovery.

As I walked away from Chason's family all I could think to myself was, *lessons and gifts. Find the lessons and the gifts.*

THE PORTAL OPENS

Stan, along with two other close Class V kayaker friends, Mike Bone and Victor Major, were using S.S. *Sexy Time* as their rescue vessel. A Z-drag system was devised across the river in the spot where Stan had last seen Chason. As in an avalanche rescue, they used a long probe and performed a grid search, stabbing at the water, hoping to land a strike.

Stan had stood witness to Chason's drowning. He did everything in his power to save his best friend, but in the end, the river had won. It was a battle no man could win alone. As redemption, Stan had to fight the battle all over again, and in doing so he gathered all the resources and manpower he could muster. With laser focus, Stan orchestrated the launch. Pointing left and then pointing right, he navigated the pulley systems until he gave them the signal to HARD STOP. With the long searching device, the men began probing at the river bottom.

Thunder began to rumble as the men made their passes through the boiling waters. My breath became short and fast, as Stan continued conducting the teams on shore to move the boat this way and that, holding the raft steady as the raging waters passed beneath it.

Just then, the men hit something. A direct strike. They had found Chason. Then, without warning, the sky began to unleash its fury and hail began raining down all around us. Time stood still as the river's currents seemed to quiet. In that moment we all felt his presence coming through. Valerie reached for my arms, but I was so caught up in the sensation of the rain that I shrugged her off, wanting to feel Chason's touch in the palms of my hands, with every droplet of water that fell from the heavens.

WHOP-BAM! CA-BOOM! A thunderclap roared above as everyone's heart skipped a beat. Chason was there. He was there, and he wanted all of us to know it. Hail beat down, prickling our skin with just enough umph to really let us know he was there. It was a *knowing*, without any of us having to express one single word. He was there, and the portal was opening. Chason was both figuratively and spiritually being released. From the river and from this realm. The sky was raining down as the portal began to open and welcome him in. He was headed to another dimension.

An unfamiliar sense of knowing rushed through my entire body. Again, I could feel the weight of grief return. My arms felt like lead, and the world began to slow down. I looked up to the heavens and watched as the thick dark clouds came pouring down. The canyon walls towering above us began to grow taller as the air all around me became thick like musk. It suddenly became difficult to breathe and I began to take quick, short breaths, in and out. My heart began to pound, palpitating at irregular beats. I could hear its rhythm reverberating in my ears.

I drew my attention back to the river and noticed a purple butterfly hovering above the spray. I looked down and noticed a caterpillar had crawled onto my foot and found a seat on my shoelace. Just inches from me, a brown trout circled in a calm eddy, mere meters from the roaring currents that held my husband's body down deep below.

As the heavens cried from above, the men in the raft began submerging themselves into the depths of the frothy Meat Grinder Rapid, while each man held onto the next man's life preserver. Their sheer will, nothing short of heroic. Gasping for air each time they breached the surface, they dove back down into the thrashing waters, wrapping Chason's body securely with ropes.

I watched as Stan began his hand gesturing again. With each signal, the raft drew closer to the safety of the shore. Back on land, the three men dispersed and got their hands on the ropes situated to pull Chason's body from his entrapment. My heart began to throb as I watched teams of friends and family line up on both sides of the river, pulling with all their might until finally one of Chason's hands emerged from the whitewater. His thick knuckles covered by his soaking wet spray top. I would know that hand anywhere. I would know those knuckles anywhere. Those were my husband's knuckles. I had just touched those fingers. I had just held that hand.

The sight of it was so disturbing that I had to find another place to focus my attention. Down below, I found the same brown trout, swimming gently in the eddy at my feet. I watched as his gills flapped back and forth. At peace in his holy place. This is how I want to picture you in your final throes. At peace in the Crystal, wild as the river flows. In an instant, my greatest fears had become my reality. I had lost Chason to the river. I had become a widow at the age of 39.

When we finally recovered his body from the Crystal, it was clear that Chason had drowned from foot entrapment. The skin and meat of his lower left calf had been stripped raw, exposing his mutilated tibia and fibula bones. Had I not been an experienced OR nurse, the sight of his leg would have sent me into complete hysterics. Instead, it brought a tremendous amount of closure. The insult to his lower left leg answered the questions that had been gnawing at me. The river had grabbed him and would not let him go.

I still needed to lay my husband's body to rest, and with special permission from the coroner, we transported Chason's body from the Crystal River to a funeral parlor in Montrose, the closest sizable town to Telluride. In my heart I knew that he needed to be brought back to the San Juans. It was where he belonged.

ASPEN HOPE

The Aspen Hope Center, a mobile crisis nonprofit who specializes in crisis intervention and suicide prevention, were the first to arrive on the scene for Chason's body recovery. As a nurse, I was familiar with the services they provide. Chason was also familiar with the organization as he had worked closely with their teams on Search and Rescue missions over the years.

When their team of certified clinicians arrived on the scene on the first day of the recovery mission, I was displaying all the classic signs of suicidal ideation. I honestly did not know how I was going to move on. My will to live was gone. I was tired of the disappointments life continued to dish out and I was feeling completely disempowered, hopeless and alone. I was at a new all-time low.

All my life, I'd lived waiting for the other shoe to drop, especially when life shined a little light my way. In those days floating down the river, freshly wed, I let my guard down. But when I got the call from Stan, I knew that not only had the other shoe dropped, but it was going to kick me in the gut while I was down.

You are not safe. Life is not safe. What a fool you were to trust. What a fool you were to think you were deserving of love. Deserving of anything good. You fool!

I was mostly unaware of their presence the first few hours beside the river that morning. When Valerie had arrived, I couldn't hold back. I unleashed all my doubts, all my disgust, and all my mistrust in the world to her.

We just got married. We just said our vows. We just got home from our honeymoon. The one time I let my guard down. The one time I felt truly happy. The one time I felt safe. Stable. Secure. The one time I allowed myself to be truly vulnerable and to feel truly relieved. The one time. And just like that. He's gone. He just fucking left me. He just fucking left!

I didn't say it out loud, but all I could think was, *I don't want to do this anymore. I don't want to be here anymore. I'm done. I don't want to live. All it will take is a bottle of tequila and a handful of pills. I have it all at home. I can end this nightmare tonight.*

As these thoughts began to plague me, I reflected on a time not so long ago that I felt all these same feelings.

Damn it. I thought I had gotten over this. I thought I had done the work. Years ago. Before Kevin died. Before I went to nursing school. I thought this hopeless narrative had worked itself out.

But this was too big. This was too much. I couldn't do it. I didn't want to live anymore.

Privy to the signs of suicidal ideation, the Aspen Hope counselors took note of my affect and assessed me as a threat to myself. After all of those years of dealing with these thoughts on my own, I found myself in a position where my suicidal ideation was no longer a secret.

The clinicians pulled Valerie aside and asked her to be my guardian for the next 72 hours. She obliged and the two of us were asked to sign a contract agreement stating: A, that I would not be alone for the next three days; and B, that I would give Aspen Hope permission to enter my home and remove anything that I could use to harm myself. This included all of Chason's guns, all of our kitchen knives, and our scissors, climbing ropes, medications, alcohol, and even cleaning agents.

I made an agreement with my family, my friends and myself that I would stay in Valerie's care until the incessant monologue of dark thoughts began to subside. I had no idea when that day would come, if ever, so I packed my bags and headed towards the one place that had always brought me solace. I was headed back to the San Juans.

CHAPTER

12

INITIATION INTO DEEP GRIEF

Being a candle is not easy; in order to give light, one must first burn.

— Rumi

'TIL DEATH DO US PART

Before Chason and I left for the courthouse on the morning of our elopement, we sat in our yoga room and held ceremony. I burned sage and blessed him. I didn't have any thoughts of warding off evil energy, as I usually do when I burn sage. I only held love in my heart.

I moved the bundle of sage around his arms, then around his legs, over his head, and under his feet. All the while, I held nothing but pure love in my heart. After we both smudged each other, I recited a prayer:

For the highest of intentions in mind.
For the best of all of those concerned.
Thank you for blessing us with such love and support.
Thank you for allowing it all to come to us with such ease and such grace.
We find gratitude in Gaia's continuous support in manifesting
all of our dreams and aspirations into reality.
Thank you for allowing space for us to think and learn and grow together.
We appreciate your guidance and inspiration, to create a more beautiful life
than either of us can ever have imagined.
Thank you, Gaia, for a life full of blessings and love.

Ceremony was held. At every step of our spiritual union. Intentions were made. I blessed Chason, and our marriage, in every way I knew how. I expressed my devoted love for him without refrain. I opened myself wholeheartedly, and he opened himself to me.

Marriage only means "as long as you both shall live." But we were not meant to spend the rest of our lives together. Instead, I later learned, we have spent many lifetimes together. Our souls, tied. To meet again in the astral and reincarnate in the physical once again, when fate deemed it fit. Now I somehow needed to find a way to honor those intentions and to honor his loss.

Grief is nothing short of paradoxical. If you allow it, you can find beauty in the face of tragedy. If you open your senses, you can stumble upon an unforeseen opportunity to learn life's greatest lessons and feel life's most profound gifts of love and support.

The flip side to grief is to fall victim to its wrath. To let it rule your emotions and stand as a catalyst to your suffering. I have seen where that path leads. I have reluctantly watched as my father has used Kevin's passing as an excuse to feed his addictions. Not me. That was not going to be my path. I was going to choose the high road. I was not going to let Chason's passing make me a victim to the story.

I did not know how, but if I was going to survive this loss, I first needed to honor Chason. I needed to make a conscious decision not to allow his passing to be in vain. *Was he a proverbial sacrifice for something bigger?* Without knowing it, I was choosing to allow Chason to be my forever teacher in this human experience.

I was changing the narrative. It didn't happen to me. It happened for me. But why? Why did he have to die? And why did I have to lose my partner in order to learn more of life's unreasonable lessons? If I was still here, on this Earth, it means I still have work to do. Chason was gone, and his legacy was my only lifeline to enduring the rough road ahead.

TAOIST MEDITATION OF WIND AND RAIN

In Chinese, the Tao signifies the way, the path, the route, the road, or sometimes more loosely, the doctrine, the principle, or holistic belief. The Tao can be roughly thought of as the flow of the Universe. It can be viewed as an essence, or a pattern, or how the natural world keeps the Universe balanced and in order.

Once I made it back to Ophir, into Valerie's guest bedroom, I arranged an emergency zoom call with Carol Grace, my longtime therapist. I was ambiguous when I made the appointment, and within minutes of our call she received the news that: A, I was married; B, I eloped; C, my husband had died; and D, that I was a widow. Carol Grace knew she needed to do something to calm my nerves as soon as she saw the mental state I was in.

A Taoist meditation came to her, and she quickly began to lead me through the exercise. I sat cross-legged on my yoga mat with my laptop in front of me. The skies were ominous and emotional that day, and I was grateful for them as they matched my mood perfectly. The monsoon season had arrived and the heavens had poured down every day since we had recovered Chason's body.

Carol's soft voice led me into a calmer state as we began to breathe together. "Raise your arms to the sky," she began. "Look up, way up, now wave your arms in circles high above your body. Take some deep breaths. In through your nose. Out through your mouth. Wave your torso back and forth, as you caress the sky with your hands."

I began finding my rhythm as I swayed back and forth with my arms raised to the heavens.

"Now bring your hands back to heart's center. Chant with me, "Hung" as you rock your body back and forth."

Together we chanted, *Hung. Hung. Hung.*

Carol's voice rose again, "Now open your heart, big and wide. Extend your arms out, now position them into cactus pose."

Still swaying to my heartbeat, I sat with my arms out in cactus.

Carol instructed, "Now chant "Hoy" as you bring your forehead to the Earth, thrusting your arms forward, keeping your arms in cactus pose."

Together we chanted, *Hoy. Hoy. Hoy.*

We repeated this over and over.

I threw my arms back into the air, circling and breathing, waving my torso from side to side. Stretching my hands out to the sky.

Then, hands back to heart center. Rocking back and forth, as if I was on a ship, chanting, *Hung. Hung. Hung.*

Then I thrust my body forward, forehead to the Earth, still chanting, *Hoy. Hoy. Hoy.*

As my third eye touched the mat, a voice came through, clear as day.

Jess, I am here. This was my ceremony. This is how it happened. This is how I came to pass. Do not fret, Dear One. Do not relive this moment over and over again in your head. I only lived it once. You do not need to relive it over and over again.

Here, I will show you how I came to pass. But then you must move forward from this.

First there was a fight. I reached for the surface, but only my hands broke through. I fought. I struggled. Then, I realized there was no escape. Breathe. No breath came. So now you breathe for me.

I looked into my heart. There you were. There all of you were. My heart. I only felt gratitude. For you. For it all.

Hung. Hung. Hung.

Then the surrender. To it all. To the river. Rushing at my back. I let it wash over me.

Hoy. Hoy. Hoy.

Relentless. Strong. Powerful. Holding me down. Holding me.

I am held. I am one with the river. I am a reed in the current.

Hoy. Hoy. Hoy.

I bowed gently, as you are now.

And so he arrived. Chason came through this Taoist Meditation. I could feel it. There was no mistake.

Just as I realized all of this, the wind began to howl. The heavens began to pour down.

"Carol," I said. "Hang on."

The window blinds begin to crash back and forth.

Thunk. Thunk. Thunk.

Rain poured into the room, and onto my computer.

Splat. Splat. Splat.

"Carol, hold on. I can't hear you over the wind and rain!" I said, scurrying off my mat to close the window and rushing to dry off my keyboard, which was now soaking wet.

"*What?!*" she exclaimed.

"A crazy squall has just blown in. The rain is pouring in. I need to shut the window!"

"Oh my!" she exclaimed. "I did not intend to do this meditation with you when you said you needed to talk. It came to me as soon as I got you on the screen. This exercise is called the Taoist Meditation of Wind and Rain!"

"Well, it certainly brought in the wind and the rain," I snarked back.

Wind and rain, I thought. *Wind and rain. Had I summoned them in? Had I summoned Chason in?*

Carol continued to explain, "When you called with your news, I had other intentions for this session. With little time to prepare, this exercise just came to me."

She sounded as surprised as I felt, and I hadn't even told her what I had experienced before the squall interrupted our session.

"Carol," I interrupted. "He came to me through our meditation. He channeled a message through you, for me. He just explained how it felt when he drowned, through these movements. He just came through, to tell me what happened."

Since his passing, I've been unable to stop perseverating on his last moments. The trauma of his drowning haunt me. *What were his last thoughts? Was he in pain? Did he suffer?*

"Carol, he just showed me. He just showed me how. He came to me as I bowed, forehead to the floor. My arms hailing in cactus pose. My third eye down to the Earth. He explained it all. It was ceremony. There was struggle. There was surrender. There was acceptance. There was beauty. There was peace. I no longer need to perseverate on the unknown. He just showed me. With every movement. With every breath. With every bow. He showed me!"

So now, when I go there, in my mind, *How did he die? What happened to him? Under that raging water?* Now I know.

Through this Taoist meditation, I now know how to breathe. I look to the heavens, arms waving, circling in the current. I find my breath. He only lived his trauma once. I do not need to relive it over and over. It has passed. A peace. A surrender. An opening of the heart.

THE BA-BOOM

Ophir is nestled at 9,850 feet. It is a small town, built during the mining days. Today it is a real life mountain hamlet, filled with families and dogs and backcountry skiers. In the summer, when the clouds roll in, temperatures drop fast. It was still raining after my therapy session with Carol Grace, but I needed some fresh air.

After the realizations I had experienced, I was rather shaken. I decided to go to the Ophir waterfall. It's a short hike through the forest, and in just a few short steps, the creek leading to the falls can make you feel far-faraway from the hustle and bustle of real life.

I stammered my way to the waterfall, set in a cauldron of loose rock and cliffs. The rains had encouraged new growth and the pines and columbine were happy for the drink. The forest was happy, and its verdant energy helped calm my nerves.

Carol Grace had told me in my therapy session that the heart chakra is green. I decided to heal myself through nature by holding hands with the pine and fir on my walk up to the waterfall. Holding space for whatever was to come through and hoping the hurt would somehow lift.

As I approached the roaring falls, I noticed how the rains had increased the flows. The waterfall was hammering down with mighty force, as I began climbing even faster up to wards the pool of rock and water.

Upon reaching the spray, I found myself experiencing an acute moment of panic. I looked up at the tendrils of water, falling down and freezing my face, and felt the magnitude and power imbued in the crag. The tranquility I'd felt just moments before, holding hands with the firs and the pines, quickly vanished, and the force of the falls shook me.

I ran out from under the landing zone of the waterfall's pool and raced up an embankment. I needed to collect myself. *What was this feeling? A feeling of terror?* It was something so powerful and yet so indescribable. It felt as though the powerful flows of the waterfall were about to kick a boulder the size of Timbuktu down onto my head, and I didn't want to be in its path.

I collected myself, then began my approach back to the base of the waterfall. I wanted to be immersed in the negative ions created by the collision of all those water and air molecules. I wanted them to fill my brain until I buzzed with sweet relief.

Instead, the mind numbing spray blasted my face with freezing cold rain. My hair blew uncontrollably, and an ice cream headache ensued. Leaning into the mist, I tried to quiet my anxious mind.

You are ok. You are safe. Nothing will hurt you here.

And that's when I felt it. Something hit me, right on the top of my head, but it was neither water nor falling rock. It felt like the reverberation of a thunderclap moving through me, from my skull to the center of my chest. My whole body seemed to shake. Almost like I'd been hit on the head with a tuning fork. It came from above, and it came with a message.

Come here, when you need me. Come here, when you need to feel me. This is where I'll be. In the cold, freezing, blowing spray. This is where I'll be. I am right here.

It was like a *Ba-boom!* above my head. Chason's vibrations entered through me via the crown chakra. He was there. With me. My face numb from the freezing cold water. My head, aching from the spray.

Come here, when you need to feel me.

It made perfect sense. This waterfall was the embodiment of Chason.

Cold. Blowing. Forceful. Powerful. Mighty. Unstoppable.

Of course this is where he would be. In the wind and the rain. The *Ba-boom* solidified the Taoist meditation experience.

Chason, a true Pisces, was now water. It was where, and how, we would communicate. This was our new love language. My senses were recalibrated that day. I was now tuned into the weather. Tuned into the flow. Tuned into the water. The life force. The onda. The ripple. The vibration. The *Ba-boom.*

MINERS' GRAVEYARD

Hidden in the dark woods of Ophir lies a sleepy miners' burial ground. A handful of lop-sided tombstones litter the lot, however not a single soul had been buried there for over a hundred years.

I was scrambling to figure out a place to lay Chason's body to rest. I informed Salli and Papa that Chason and I had discussed what we would like done, in the case that one of us died. I told them that Chason was adamant about becoming one with the earth and did not want to be cremated.

It seemed appropriate to bury him at the Observatory, but after much discussion with Papa, Salli and Garrett, we decided burying Chason on that piece of land would be a challenge. The hut is a vacation rental and it would be awkward visiting the site while people were there, deep in the mountains, enjoying the scenery. Valerie mentioned that Ophir might be the perfect spot. The graveyard had just recently been surveyed and was ready for people to purchase plots.

From where Chason would lie, he would be able to keep close watch as we skied the robust terrain that surrounded him. It served as a vantage point. The perfect place to lay a man devoted to mountain search and rescue to rest.

After walking through the abandoned cemetery with Valerie and Garrett and choosing an exact location, I decided to take a solo walk to the waterfall. It felt weird making all these big decisions without him. I was hoping that a quick chat with the spray would give me the confirmation I so desperately needed.

Who knew marriage would look like this? I would have never guessed that marrying Chason would have meant making all these end-of-life decisions so soon.

As the mist cleansed my body, I allowed the negative ions to fill my head and heart. I sat and watched as the tiny tendrils of water fell to the ground. Over and over again, my eyes followed the falling droplets. Weak hydrogen bonds permeated the atmosphere around me, and their erratic motion put my nervous system at ease. My shaking hands and tight chest began to relax.

Will you be happy here? Would this be the place you'd want to be laid to rest? Why do I have to make all these decisions alone? Why did you have to leave me so soon? Why did you have to go kayaking? You just left me. You just fucking left me!

As I turned away from the falling water, the rocks of the gorge began to play tricks on my eyes. Just as the water appeared to be falling down, the rocks appeared to be rising up. Nothing made sense. Nothing in my periphery was standing still. The ground underneath me became unstable, and my legs began to buckle. An intense urgency came over me and before I could understand what was happening, I found myself screaming at the top of my lungs. Like I was trying to extract some horrible being from my innards.

A bellow, so frightening, burst out of my lungs. My hands began to tremble again; my body began to shake. Just as quickly as the primal scream left my body, tears began pouring down, soaking me quicker than the mists of the falls.

Was this all an illusion? Was I just a cast member in some horrible melodramatic play? What did I do to deserve this?

THE BARDO

I scheduled an acupuncture appointment with a powerful herbal practitioner the morning before visiting Chason's body at the funeral parlor. I was hopeful that his healing powers would give me the strength and energy I needed for what I'd be facing that day.

I lay on the table in complete and utter adrenal fatigue. As he placed the thin needles around my heart and lungs, I felt the exhaustion leave my body. Then he strategically placed dabs of mugwort around my navel and lit the spongy herb until the leaves stimulated my Qi.

Then he performed a ceremony for Chason's spirit, chanting the Tibetan Buddhist mantra *Om Benzra Satto Hum Tadyatha Hane Hane Anoli Mitaye Guruye Benzra Satto Svaha.* He chanted this mantra 108 times, and then asked me, when the ceremony was complete, if I had ever heard of *The Tibetan Book of the Dead* that describes the bardo, the transitional period between death and either rebirth or liberation. I said I'd heard of it, but needed to know more about the ceremony he was performing.

In the *Book of the Dead,* he explained, rebirth is part of *samsara*—the cycle of birth, death, and rebirth—that we all experience as living, breathing humans. In the bardo, if one is to transcend *samsara*, one will experience liberation from those cycles into the ultimate state of nirvana.

By definition, he said, we are always walking through transitional states of the bardo, even here on Earth. It's a liminal state, much like when you travel on an airplane from one city to another, packed into a tube, flying tens of thousands of feet above the Earth, neither here nor there. And while you aren't doing much to get from here to there, you eventually do get somewhere. And while you are sitting in that tube, doing nothing, much is happening.

For 49 days after their passing, the acupuncturist said, the deceased exist in this liminal state. It is a journey where the light of their life begins to fade away completely, while the light of the next life has not yet appeared.

He then explained that while the deceased lie in their dying slumber, a monk will read to them from the *Tibetan Book of the Dead*, guiding them through their journey.

Do not resist. Do not be afraid. Fill your heart with compassion and let your mind be at ease. The four great elements of your body are collapsing now, one into the other, as if you are being crushed by mountains, tossed by waves, scorched and carried off by a strong wind.

This is the bardo of the dying. It is important now to recognize your own true nature. Do not resist this. Do not be afraid. Rest in this. The vast empty luminosity of the mind itself. Watch as the earth collapses into water. And water collapses into fire. Fire into air, and watch in wild wonder as air dissolves into consciousness.

Then experience the piercing luminosity, the pure white light, the clear radiance that arises from the direct experience of one's own basic nature. Now there is no darkness, now there is no separation. No direction and no shape. Only brilliant light.

This boundless sparkling radiance is mind, free from the shadows of birth and death, free from boundaries of any kind. Now all pervasive light engulfs you completely, all of space has dissolved into pure light, this radiance is the mind of all Buddhas, of all the awakened ones. To recognize this, is all that is necessary to transcend. To liberate yourself. To escape samsara, and live eternally in nirvana.

I walked out of the session feeling lighter and freer than I had since I'd left the pixie dust fairy on the shores of the Crystal River. I felt more clear, more enlightened. Like he had somehow pressed a reset button for my mind, body and soul, using only his needles and his prayers.

AHA'S ON THE UNCOMPAHGRE

After being in the river for two days and then being placed in a refrigerator for several more, Chason's body had begun to decompose more quickly than the morticians had anticipated. After I visited his body in Montrose, I felt a desperate and urgent need to get him into the ground as quickly as possible.

On my way home from the funeral parlor, I decided to wash away the odor of decay by submerging myself in the Uncompahgre River. I had been ruminating on Chason's body being held at the bottom of the river for two days, and now I couldn't escape the guilt of leaving him in a refrigerator for many more. After witnessing his current state, I knew that he needed to be buried sooner rather than later.

As I leaned into the shockingly cold hold of the Unc's current, I had a moment that left me feeling held, and also at peace. As my right ear began to ring, Chason whispered softly,

It was ceremony. My time in the river. It was ceremony. I needed those days, in its grip, to become one with its forces. One with the river. One with its rage. One with its currents. My body felt it. My soul needed it. So long that my very essence was washed away. Confluencing downstream with the mighty Colorado, Where our hearts will meet again. It was all meant to be, and it was meant for me. It was ceremony. Thank you for allowing me that time. Time to become one with the river.

Just then a stick, gnawed once by a beaver, grazed the palm of my hand. I gripped it, hoping to hold on a little longer to what was already slipping past. It was brief, but it was *a knowing*. It was *an all-telling*.

Chason was meant to be in the river. It was part of his own bardo experience. I did not need to feel the weight of that burden any longer. I no longer needed to feel bogged down with guilt. It was okay. He was okay. It was where he was supposed to be.

It was a body recovery that was meant to be. A mission that needed to be executed. He was there to experience it all. The skill. The strength. The power. The knowledge. The determination. The courage. He was there for it all. And he let us know by pouring rain and hail down on us that day.

It was paradoxical. The tragedy and beauty were palpable. Both disheartening and awe-inspiring. Chason's passing offered everyone he loved so deeply the opportunity to show up as their best selves.

I drove to Chason's parents' house to explain my concern about his decomposing state at the funeral parlor. I was adamant that we bury him sooner than later. His family was still not completely sold on my plan about burying him in the Ophir Cemetery.

In the heat of this emotional debate, a fleet of F-16 fighter jets began to thunder above. I raced out of the house to catch the squadron as another low-flying fighter flew past. The reverberation of the powerful jet sent me to my knees. I could feel its force, and for the second time that day I was rocked to my core.

Chason was obsessed with flying. He was reading a pilot's instructional manual each night before bed. It could not have been a drier read, nor could it have been a more obvious sign. Chason wanted out of the fridge and into the ground. And it was going to happen that night.

OH FOR THE LOVE OF GOD, OPHIR

Six months prior to Chason's passing, we received news that one of our friends had been buried in an avalanche. It was a devastating loss, as he had just become a father to identical twin boys. Days prior to his accident, Chason and I had skinned up Aspen Highlands Ski Resort with him. He couldn't have been a prouder dad, showing us pictures of his two baby boys as we made our way up the mountain.

The day of the accident, our friend was out on a hall pass, doing some backcountry skiing on the Battleship, a mountain just north of Ophir. He was skiing with a colleague, and the two were slated to meet up with their wives afterward for a fancy dinner out on the town. It would have been the couple's first date night since having their twins. The babysitter was all lined up and the wives were ready to go, but the two skiers never came home that night.

On their second lap skinning up the mountain, a slide was triggered. Neither of them survived. The twins were just seven weeks old.

Chason and I had a conversation shortly after our friend passed. We were discussing the choices our friend had made that day, which led to a deeper discussion. I told Chason that he too would have to start rearranging his priorities, now that we were getting married and trying to have a baby.

"If you die," I said, "your passing won't affect you at all. Because you will be dead. It will be me and your mom and your dad and your brother and all the rest of us who will have to deal."

I asked that he consider me when he was out in those exposed and risky situations. I asked that he prioritize me, so that we could always ski or paddle another day together. It was not a light conversation by any stretch of the imagination, as we both knew the mountains giveth and the mountains taketh away.

We decided to make a password list that day. For many reasons. Chason's lifestyle was dangerous. Mountain Rescue put him in dangerous situations, and his hunger for skiing big mountains and paddling Class V rapids made this homework assignment even more of a priority. He took this project very seriously and made a list of all his accounts and passwords. He showed me his work, and I showed him mine, then we filed the papers away.

Moments after we recovered Chason's body from the river, I remember a close friend asking me what I planned to do with his body. Another friend interjected, saying, "Well, he'd probably want to be cremated." Chason definitely did not want to be cremated, I told them. He wanted a natural burial.

He had seen something on social media about a tree pod burial. The pod encapsulates you in a mushroom spore–filled sac, and you become fertilizer for a tree that is later planted above. We had just discussed it.

Unfortunately, when I tried ordering the shroud, I was told that it would take six weeks to arrive. Turns out you have to plan for things like that to be delivered. I decided to pivot.

The gardener in me wanted to simply wrap Chason in weed barrier and chicken wire. I thought this approach was the most pragmatic and would be something Chason would agree upon. But as I told this idea to two of my dearest friends, I watched as horror spread across their faces. I decided it was probably not the best idea, for all of those concerned, and that it would probably not go over so well with his parents, so again, I pivoted.

Two of my oldest and dearest friends, Tanya and Mason, began devising Plan C. Tanya was able to find a linen ceremonial wrap from an eco-friendly burial service that could be shipped overnight.

Mason agreed that Chason's body should be protected from the animals and began researching alternatives. He found an old toboggan litter that was once used by a local mountain rescue team back in the day.

Both the linen cloth and rickety old toboggan weren't far from my weed barrier and chicken wire ideas. In fact the toboggan was lined with something very similar to chicken fencing and the linen shroud was even more durable and more cleverly designed than the mushroom pod.

Valerie called in a favor with the EMS crew that she worked with. She arranged to have a refrigerator truck deliver Chason from the funeral parlor in Montrose to the burial site in Ophir. An old friend offered his services and dug a hole in the cemetery with his back hoe and within twenty four hours we had devised a burial plan. We would do an intimate burial on the evening of June 30th, with only a few close family members and friends. Then we would have a more formal burial ceremony and memorial, the following day up on Wilson Mesa.

NOW I LAY THEE DOWN TO SLEEP

I had my friend position Chason's grave so that he looked towards the east, the direction of the rising sun. He was a believer in the directional alignments in the ancient Vastu Shastra texts. Buddha found enlightenment facing east; therefore, even our bed at home faced east. I remember him drawing on a cocktail napkin how our bed would be positioned in the dream house we were planning to build. He'd be eternally upset if I hadn't considered these important details for his final resting place.

After my friend had finished digging the hole with his backhoe, I sat in the grave that would house my dead husband and I prayed. I prayed for his soul. I prayed that I would survive the heartbreak. I prayed for a future where we would meet again. I prayed that he would show me the way. And I prayed that both Chason and I would find peace with what had transpired.

As his hole was being dug, a giant rock was unearthed, and the depression it left made a perfect shelf for a miniature shrine. I placed a bible, a pocket watch, and a rosary in the sacred space: mementos from his Italian and Irish ancestral lineages, given to me earlier by Salli and Papa. They chose not to come up to Ophir the night of Chason's actual burial. It was too difficult for them to witness. I hoped the tokens would bring Chason good fortune on the other side.

An old friend and work colleague had given me a woven basket filled with herbs and infusions used in biodynamic planting ceremonies. She and I had spent three summers together, building soil, brewing compost, and planting a beautiful biodynamic garden together at the yoga center in Carbondale, and I knew that she had put great thought into the contents of the basket.

Her care package was unlike any other. It was more of a ceremonial burial package, comprising all of the right herbs and potions for the rites I was about to perform. It was filled with everything I could think of to properly place Chason's body into the ground while nourishing the soil and plants above.

I burnt palo santo, fireweed, white sage, lavender, and sweet grass. I did a ceremonial rub from a bushel of mesa sage harvested from our neighborhood in Woody Creek. I smudged the space, cleansing it of any negative energy, and then invited in all the positive energy that I could muster.

I sprinkled dried rose hips and mullen harvested from our backyard. I spread manure that had been carefully packaged in a cow's horn and buried for a full season before it was given to me to be rubbed into the deep dark earth. I baptized the soil with essence of frankincense and myrrh, and I held space for Chason's energy to transition into his next stage.

Arnica was going off that summer, growing prolifically in the mountains surrounding Ophir. Valerie harvested an entire bag of the medicinal flower while I was holding space in the grave. When she arrived with her yield, I immersed myself in its bounty. The fresh aroma was sweet and was the perfect antidote to the smells of death and decay that I had experienced at the funeral parlor.

Val and I covered the earth with the heart-shaped leaves and golden blossoms until the floor of the grave was glowing yellow. A pair of Steller's jays circled and squawked, as we felt the medicines begin to nourish the space.

The monsoons had come early that year, and the clouds hung low, playing tricks on our eyes as their mists passed through the spires of North and South Lookout Peaks. As I exited the grave, I looked out towards the west and saw an indescribable orb of light glowing just below Sunshine Peak. It was a holy radiance, and I immediately felt his presence.

People began to arrive. "He's here," I said to the crowd of intimate friends that had begun to congregate.

Minutes later, the refrigerator truck that was carrying my husband arrived. As it turned off its engine, I looked over towards the east as an ephemeral prism began to show its ROY-G-BIV colors.

"No rainbows," I said in a low stern voice.

It didn't feel appropriate for the striking light to distract me from the moody clouds that were engulfing us. I wasn't feeling jovial in the least, and the good fortune and luck that normally accompany a rainbow was not welcome in this moment of deep sorrow. The ephemeral rainbow disappeared as quickly as it had arrived.

As I finished wishing away the prism, I turned towards the cold bed of the delivery truck to retrieve my husband's body. Before I had Chason's body transported to Ophir I had the mortician wrap his body in the ceremonial burial shroud that Tanya had overnighted. It encased him like a mummy. I had the mortician adorn his body with crystals and arrowheads that he had collected on his worldly travels, over the course of his lifetime.

Collectively we carried him, and as we walked him up the steep embankment to his final resting place I remember thinking, never in a million years could I have ever foreseen myself being a huckle bearer to my newly wedded husband.

Using the straps tied into his burial shroud, we lowered his body into the freshly dug hole.

"You are held. You are held," were the only words that came to me, so I chanted them over and over until his body was safely lowered into the ground.

Once we laid him down to rest, we covered him with the old retired toboggan litter. As we began to shovel dirt into the hole, I began arranging large rocks that Chason had collected into arrays resembling the seven chakras. Each layer of dirt covering his body was gilded with the healing artifacts he had spent a lifetime collecting.

BRISTLECONE PINE

One year later, the mound of soil that covered Chason's body had settled. The straw that we had laid over the raw dirt had receded and wild lupine and dandelion began to sprout. I planted a young bristlecone pine sapling at the foot of Chason's resting place. Bristlecones were native to the Ophir Valley before the miners stripped the land over a hundred years ago. With a lifespan of thousands of years, the tree seemed the most appropriate symbolic testament to Chason's legacy. A natural marker among the prayer flags and other tokens left behind by friends and family.

The bristlecone pine is one of the most resilient trees on the planet, growing in some of the world's most harsh environments, in poor soils, and under some of the most undesirable conditions. This is how I felt. That my own personal growth must flourish in this harsh new undernourished and undesirable environment. I needed to embody the resilience of the bristlecone pine if I was going to survive this loss.

After I planted, fed, and watered the tree, I couldn't help but see myself in its twisted gnarl. A perfect representation of all the emotions I'd been feeling. My stomach in knots. My mind a torrent of thoughts. My body aching with emotion. I found myself in yet another fit of rage. I raised my fists to the sky and moaned out a primal scream of rage.

As the bellow left my lungs, I looked up to the heavens and thought to myself, *If I choose to end this life, I will have to relive all of these experiences all over again. In order to overcome this, you must rise above it all. Honor this loss. Do not let his passing be in vain. Lift the veil of shame and tell your story so others in the depths of their own grief do not have to feel the isolation you are feeling every living day of this god-forsaken life.*

Then I asked myself, *What would Chason want me to do? How would he want me to move forward?*

He would often say to me, "I just want you to do what makes you happy." That is what he would want me to do. Do what makes me happy.

But how could I feel happiness with him gone, and with so many of my demons back to haunt me? I had so much to sort through before I could start to feel the light again. That's when a mantra entered my mind: *A hurting heart is a holy heart.* I thought to myself, *Write about that.*

With pen and paper, I began working out the emotions running through my heart. While thoughts of ending my life plagued me, the realization of what that would do to my family and friends continually stopped me from acting. When the hurt felt like too much to tolerate, I sought refuge in my pen. The process helped me better understand myself and allowed me the space and time to find meaning in the loss.

At times, the shame and discomfort that came with these dark thoughts felt unmanageable. But I knew I had to share my experience. If Chason's legacy was outdoor education, than mine was going to be awareness around suicidal ideation. All I could think was that, if by sharing my story, I was able to bring solidarity to another in their time of crisis, then that's what I must do.

As I grieve my husband and learn to live without him, I have become focused on the epidemic of mental illness and suicide in the mountains. The State of Colorado is ranked the tenth highest in suicide rates among all 50 states. So often mental illness goes hand in hand with tragedy. Far too often people suffer in silence. I share this story in hopes of lifting the veil of shame that surrounds suicidal ideation and connecting on a level that nurtures the grieving process.

It is so important to recognize the signs and symptoms of suicidal ideation. If you suspect that someone you know is having suicidal thoughts, do not shy away from the topic. Ask them directly, "Are you having thoughts of harming yourself?" This is a very compassionate and direct question to ask. It can be uncomfortable, but it is a conversation we all must get more comfortable having. It may very well save a life. Shedding light on this subject certainly continues to save mine.

If this speaks to you, please know that you are not alone in your struggle. It takes a lot of energy to be strong. You cannot do it alone. Please seek help if these dark thoughts are plaguing you.

Your experience
Is a manifestation
Of your projection

Every expression
From you is a reflection
Of my truest self

Epilogue

Eight days of marriage was all the time that Chason and I were given. They were the best eight days of my life. But time is not linear. And if time is not linear, then Chason and I will meet again, and we will live many more lifetimes together. I believe this to be true, because he is a part of me, our souls tied. And until we meet again, I will continue to love him infinitely.

The Ancient Greeks had eight words to describe the depths of love:

Eros, a romantic, passionate love;
Philia, an intimate, authentic friendship;
Erotoropia, a playful, flirtatious love;
Storge, an unconditional and familial love;
Philautia, compassionate self-love;
Pragma, a committed, companionate love;
Agápe, empathetic, universal love;
And *mania*, much like in the English language, an obsessive love.

I like to think that I've experienced all eight of these depths of love for Chason. But I wish there was also a word to describe how I feel today. A word that describes my appreciation and gratitude for all the adversity that I have experienced. Because words like acceptance, fortitude and resilience just don't cut it.

Kintsugi is the Japanese word used to describe the beauty that can be found in the broken. The word is a combination of two words. *Kin*, meaning *gold*, and *tsugi*, meaning *to join together*. A clay bowl is not discarded, but painstakingly mended by the patient potter's hands, welded back together with inlays of powdered gold. The finished product becomes more beautiful than its original form.

This is how I feel today, *kintsugi'd*, and somehow grateful for being broken open by the loss of Chason. It's given me a newer perspective and a wider barometer of how to feel. It has allowed me the ability to learn about all of the emotions that I continue to experience. I try to do my best to honor each and every one of these emotions as they show up. And in allowing myself to feel them, and name them, I also try to be compassionate with myself when I am in my darkest hours. I guess this is what it means to be truly alive. To truly feel. And although I do not necessarily want to live each and every day, I continue to get out of bed and see what the day may bring. Like a needlepoint that once hung in my mother's living room said, *The Present Is A Gift, Untie The Ribbons.*

Acknowledgements

As Chason asked me to do while writing our vows, I will continue to write my acknowledgements. First I'd like to thank him for being present on every phone call I made to all of his mentors and childhood friends. I was hesitant at first when I decided to ask for help. I needed more insight about the events that took place before, during and after I had met him. Sometimes we just don't get enough time with the ones we love to ask them all the questions we'd like to, in order to get to know them better. Thank you for sharing your stories with me Galena Gleason, Pam East, Bill Glasscock, Annie Quathamer and Brian O'Neill.

Each time I got on the phone with one of them, a rainbow would appear, thunderclaps would rumble, and rain and wind would join in on the conversation. A tornado even touched down the morning I sent my manuscript to my mother and sister in Eden, New York. All these weather events confirmed that I was on the right path telling this story, and gave me the strength and courage I needed to carry on.

Next I'd like to thank all the friends and family who came to sit with me on the river those days during the recovery, and all those many months later. Without your love and support, I would have chosen to leave this world, on my own terms and of my own volition. For all of you who have sent me healing prayers, I am deeply grateful for your positive energy.

Thank you to my Mom, Lori Lockwood, my Aunt Mary Gavin, Elizabeth Vaughan, Dave Vaughan, Michael Lockwood, Heather Osborne, Aadyn Lockwood, Gabriel Lockwood, Salli and Jim Russell, Garrett Russell, G.Love, Kathleen Weber, Jody Gavin, The Gavin Family, The Lockwood Family, Valerie Hill Sloan, Dylan Sloan, Ryah Sloan, Joaquin Sloan, Gary and Debbie Hill, Carley and Amanda Hill, Hilary Popper Swenson, Kyle Swenson, Duke Swenson, Talina Swenson, Tanya Paliani, John Neubert, Brad Zaporski, Mason and Matty Rich, Biggie and Ruthie Rich, Stan Prichard, Cat Leonaitis, McKinley Hale, Jeremy Womack, Caci Grinspan, Kate Danaher, Erin Mitchell, Adam Malgram, Sydney Schalit, Michael Hayes, Meg and Molly Olenick, JF Bruegger, Johnny Rossman, Jenny Ryden Harris, Will Cardamone, Jordan and Elizabeth White, Willy and Sara Volkhoussen, Claire Noone, Alex Claydon, Allison Daily, Carol Grace, Josh Geter, Joe Hummel, John Bukolt, Emily Brown, Julie Hassey, Kara Caldwell, Daniel and Vanessa Boldt, Allyn and Christina Logan, Dave Bumgardener, Holden Scott, Eeliyana Paraiso, Ashley Jardine, Joanna Klebes, Lindsey Jackson, Josh and Rachee Williams, Brad Foley, Kimmy Grant, Jeremy Yanko, Steven Steinberg, Steve Rubenstein, Kathleen and Ryan Bonneau, Casey Graves and Joel Lee, Emily Scott, Cher Aslor and Mat Ryan, Mike Doherty, Paige Breslford, Casey Franklin, Caroline Richardson, Parke and Ryan Ehlers, Jacey DePriest and Travers Mitchell, Sue and Dan Hehir, Cynthia Zehm, Gina Guarascio Murdock, Lisa Ball, Naani Sheva, Megan Miller, Koral DellaTierra, Lisa Chism, Ody Loomis, Erin Hicks, Lisa "Beast" Dickenson, Rebecca Mirsky, Andrew Helsley, George Kuckly, Simon and Kimberly Collins, Claudia and Cruise Quenelle, Emily Morgan Nevin, Sean Nevin, Christofer and Fiona Drew, Deanna, Pat, Wylee and Gunnar Drew, Virginia Drew, Josh Borof, Andy and Kara Bagnall, Brian Gavin, Victor Major, Mike Bone, Orion Helms, Lander Gillies, Brian Conlin, Hallie Coulter, Jesse Peckela, Sheila Finey, Angela Mallord, Bob and Penelope Gleason, Ryan Howe, Erin Raley Wilson and Matt Wilson, and to all the Buffalo, Telluride and Roaring Fork communities who loved both Chason and I.

I'd like to thank Kelley McMillan Manley, who believed in me, and Elizabeth Hightower Allen, my mentor and editor, who saw the potential in my collection of short stories and helped me navigate the waters of piecing together this telling of love and loss. I'd also like to thank the Carbondale Fire Department for offering our tribe a headquarters for the recovery of Chason's body. I'd also like to thank Mountain Rescue Aspen for offering their expertise in the recovery, as well as the Aspen Hope Center and the Pathfinders Grief Counselors for being by my side.

Lastly, I would like to thank all those whom I have loved and lost. Without our deep connection, friendship, and love, my heart would not know what it means to truly live. Your spirits are alive in me, and for that I am grateful. Thank you, James and Betty Gavin, Kevin Lockwood, Shawn Gavin, Matthew Gannon, David Buckley, James "Whipper" Snyder, Rick Sievert, Brian Moore, David Gugino, Nick McNamara, Bill Pierce, Steve Sullivan, Nate Flick, Christie Kellerman, Justin Mach, Matt Gonser, Mike Carrow, Hilary Fitzgerald, Wiley Wood, Clark Wine, Rob Liberman, Steve Root, Gabe Wright, Lindsey Welch, Hannah Smith, Devin Overton, Richard Zehm, Hilaree Nelson, Lani Jones, Bridget Malone, Michael Gardner, and most of all, Chason Russell.

SPREAD THE LOVE

A portion of the proceeds from the sale of this book will go to the Chason Russell Memorial Foundation at the Telluride Academy; the Kevin Patrick Lockwood Memorial Fund, which awards kids with educational and recreational opportunities; as well as to the Aspen Hope Center, a mobile crisis intervention outreach program and suicide prevention resource; and Pathfinders Grief Counseling, a support network that aids the friends and families of those who are terminally ill, or who have passed.

If you'd like to donate to the Kevin Patrick Lockwood Memorial Fund please visit:

Facebook at the Kevin P. Lockwood Memorial Fund

If you 'd like to further Chason's legacy in outdoor education please visit:

https://tellurideacademy.org/chason-p-russell-memorial-fund/

If you'd like to donate to the Aspen Hope Center please visit:

https://www.aspenhopecenter.org/donate

If you'd like to donate to Pathfinder's Grief Counseling please visit:

https://www.pathfindersforyou.org/support-us